The biggest challenge ever is to be an ordinary man

- Lucio Dalla - Italian Singer

Disclaimer

The information in this book is meant to supplement, not replace, proper desert training. Like any sport involving extreme environment , equipment, balance and environmental factors, extreme desert exploration poses some inherent risk. The author advise readers to take full responsibility for their safety and know their limits. Before practicing the skills described in this book, be sure that your physical training and equipment is well maintained, and do not take risks beyond your level of experience, aptitude, training, and comfort level.

INTRODUCTION

Breaking record after record, an Italian man is getting ready to face the last obscure piece of land in the heart of the harshest and unexplored desert in the world; the Empty Quarter (Rub al Khali) in Saudi Arabia. It is a 1,200 km desert of sand and nothing but sand. Entering the mind-set of this expert of extreme desert exploration you will be stunned by this brave adventurer who could make Sir Edmund Hillary's conquest of Everest or Neil Armstrong's walk on the moon seem like nothing in comparison. Max Calderan is a well-known name in the Arabian Peninsula, and numerous articles have been written about him. In 2014, the Qatari Al-Jazeera broadcasting station dedicated a special documentary about him and broadcasted it worldwide. He has been welcomed by presidents, ministers and high-ranking authorities in the Arab world. International newspapers and TV stations have dedicated space to his feats and challenges of 'alleged limits' of the human body, in a territory where even Bedouins and herders are not able to resume their activities in its blazing heat.

Technology is important, says Max, but when you get in the heat of the action, the only thing to do is to pray and ask for help from God and certainly not from the pair of shoes you are wearing. "I do not want to die, and I feel ready for doing something that no-one else has ever thought of doing before, simply because the challenge was considered impossible from the onset: impossible to go where no other human being in living memory has ever been to. Then, to our surprise we discover that there are no limits beyond man's power."

Max's feats are just one long embrace with the point of no

return.

Max's body temperature is over 41 degrees, his blood pressure is 70 over 30 (Max Calderan does not expect any medical assistance, and he monitors all parameters by himself).

After all, he is an extreme explorer, an expert of the desert and has a philosophy that does not leave room for any doubt. As a matter of fact, his project is called "Redefine the Extreme". Max is the only person who is able to stand the desert in the very middle of summer when temperatures soar to the highest worldwide. Max can face the desert in this way:

- through self-sufficiency of food and water;
- without any external help whatsoever;
- without any medical or technical assistance;
- running non-stop (night and day);
- by micro-nap sleeping;
- by never following tracks, roads, or paths which have previously trodden by other humans;
- even in the very middle of summer (in heats of over 58 degrees).

"I wanted to do something that no man had ever done before, go where no-one else had ever gone, undertake challenges that nobody would have repeated, at all. I wanted to break through the absolute limit so I could tell everybody loud and clear You, too, are able to do this because no-one can stop you from chasing your dreams. You are far stronger and more powerful than what you think and believe you are."

Max performed some of his most important feats (ranked first in the world) in the middle of summer and here is a short summary of those:

April 2006: Qatar. He crossed the longest diagonal line from the border with Saudi Arabia up to the Arabian Gulf: 202 kilometres non-stop in 38 hours.

January 2007: Oman. He became the first man in the world to follow the imaginary line of the Tropic of Cancer, covering 437 kilometres from the United Arab Emirates' border to the Gulf of Oman, in 90 hours and 20 minutes.

August 2007: Wahiba Sands desert in Oman. He became the first man in the world to cover 200 kilometres in 48 hours in the very middle of summer (+56 ° C) when even Bedouins themselves rest due to the excessive heat.

August 2008: Oman. Summer double run at Sharqiya Sands. He covered 360 kilometres in a total of 75 hours. Peak temperature was about 58 degrees. Max covered the whole track, from East to West and from North to South, in two separate sessions. In the second session he ran out of water, doing without for 22 hours while covering 160 kilometres. The Bedouins could not believe their eyes when they saw Max Calderan disappear, only to re-emerge again, having been swallowed by the scorching sands.

May 2009: Palestine-Sinai. A 315 km run in total which was a double challenge in a desert with a human soul and a land which has been immortalised by the Bible. The aim of his run was to carry a strong message of peace and togetherness amongst the people, thus the name "The Run for Love". After his official meeting with the Palestinian President Abu Mazen, Max set off from Ramallah (The West Bank) and crossed Jerusalem to reach Gaza, having covered 105 km. At an Israeli check-point, Max came to learn what having a gun-machine pointed at you, ready to be fired, means. Following that, after a short transfer, he resumed his run and crossed the Sinai Desert in Egypt to cover other 210 kilometres in which he opened a new path, under the incredulous eyes of the Bedouin tribes. This challenge had been written in the Sacred Book of Canun, kept at Saint Catherine's Monastery at the foot of Mount Sinai.

August 2009: Yemen. Just as Max was about to cover 450 kilometres across the Ramlat Al-Sabatayn Desert, alleged terrorists, who were affiliated to Al-Qaeda, were arrested twelve hours before Max was due to start his run. The terrorists were arrested at the very point that Max wanted to reach which obliged Max to postpone his run to a safer, future date.

August 2010: The Sinai Peninsula in Egypt. Max crossed the 154 km length of the Tih Desert from south to north in almost 25 hours. Some Bedouins who live on its higher plains have never seen the sea nor the rain.

December 2010: The Sinai Peninsula in Egypt. Max ran 148 km in 23 hours and 50 minutes, covering the area from Abu Zenima on the Red Sea to Saint Catherine at the foot of Mount Sinai, thus following the footsteps of Moses' biblical exodus. The team that was supposed to welcome him at a certain check-point, did not see him arriving and began a search for him. They later discovered that he had already got through its narrow passages and labyrinths at an impressive speed hours before.

August 2011: United Arab Emirates, on the border with Saudi Arabia, near the historic Liwa Oasis. He defied his body resistance by not eating nor drinking for 24, 36, and 48 hours, and solely running non-stop across the 200 km of sand where the scorching temperature was over 74 degrees Celsius.

August 2012: Crossing the Sinai Desert coast to coast, covering 250 km in 48 hours from the Gulf of Suez to the Gulf of Aqaba. Al-Jazeera cameras followed Max and witnessed him complete another astonishing feat without drinking or eating from sunrise to sunset during the month of Ramadan. Al-Jazeera produced a documentary about Max's impressive experience which was broadcasted all over the world. Al Jazeera published articles about Max's experience on its home page for ten days in a row, together with the most important international front page news.

December 2012: Saudi Arabia and his first official attempt to cross the Empty Quarter. Max set off from Najran on the border with Yemen, but a very harsh sandstorm made him have to stop after having run only 270 km (the dunes shifted by 80 meters in 24 hours).

Afterwards, he remarked "... in those moments, one eats sand, breathes sand and spits sand..."

June 2003: Jesolo, Italy. A non-stop climb of a flight of 77 thousand stairs in 24 hours, to raise money for a charity event.

Fourteen stairs to climb up, then along three meters of horizontal ramp and back down fourteen stairs. He walked 130,000 steps to cover a distance of 15,500 meters of a totally uneven land. So unrelenting.

Max Calderan would never throw in the towel. He is an unyielding believer. He believes that we can change what we call 'world': that world that we create around ourselves in an attempt to be happy and fulfilled. His journeys have become a message he writes one step after another with his footprints on the sand.

Max Calderan considers the "Redefining the Extreme" project as a way to take man back to his origins and roots when he used to roam alone for hundreds of kilometres, having very little food and water at his disposal. Starting from the Homo Sapiens, our ancestors used to travel to far off places and probably had only short naps for fear of being devoured by beasts.

In this perspective, the project, which began in 2006, will end with a great challenge that will bridge the last remaining gap in the story of land exploration with an attempt to cross the last largely unexplored place on our planet; a place of sand and mystery where the Bedouins would not risk going, even if accompanied by the most expert guides, for a fear so great that even their camels dare not tread there. It is a place from which migratory birds swerve away and oil companies are unable to fully access.

This place is the desert of the Empty Quarter (Rub Al Khali) in Saudi Arabia (a 1200 km journey in total). This challenge had already been undertaken without success in 2012. It is the biggest sand desert in the world, and Max is going to cross through its central part, thus connecting the two most extreme points.

Max Calderan says: "The secret of Life is precisely here. It is from this point that Man began discovering the world and it is not by chance that this land is the only place on Earth that is completely uncontaminated by humans."

He expresses his reaction to death in the emotional balance he has reached. Once, he was asked "What would you do if you felt that death is imminent?" He answered candidly by replying "I would certainly not despair. I am trained for avoid her..."

Max's confidence and peacefulness in dealing with difficulties developed in adolescence while already an extreme athlete of climbing sports and extreme ski-mountaineering.

His endeavours were fulfilled when he was awarded a Medal of Civil Valour by the President of the Republic, for being the winner of the Pentathlon military national championships and for having graduated with the highest honours in Sports Science, after having presented an experimental thesis which was subsequently published in a prestigious scientific American magazine.

He has been the manager of a multinational pharmaceutical company, trainer and entrepreneur. In his private life, he has gone through tremendously difficult times both professionally and emotionally. " I qualify myself to make remarks because what I speak about are experiences which I have been through, some of which were dramatic. Instead of surrendering, crying, and despairing, I transformed those difficulties into opportunities in order to test myself, without having to be thankful to anybody, apart from God."

"This is my goal now: to make as many people as possible aware of their greatness and their huge untapped potential waiting to be developed by using all the instruments that technology and commonsense have put at our disposal. But, before all of that, let usexploit ourselves. Let us ask ourselves what we are doing to improve the world and to fight evil and injustice which dominate us. Let us first improve ourselves so that the world can benefit. I am a believer not a dreamer! I am not mad for crossing desolate inaccessible deserts. Fools are those who do nothing to change the world or themselves, who only complain and shuffle away their responsibilities by off-loading them onto other people's shoulders.

EVERYTHING IS CLEAR
IF WE WANT TO OPEN YOUR EYES

Few people are aware of it and even fewer are those who grasp it. It is the Big Deception; the biggest fraud that has ever been masterminded, involving us all. It continues to stealthily perpetrate, slyly and deeply wedging itself into our minds so deeply that it is mingled with our DNA, giving birth to hybrid thoughts, hybrid actions, and hybrid offspring. This happens by undermining God's laws, or, for the unbelievers, by undermining the laws of an origin, which as you may put it, is common to all.

The Big Deception is within ourselves when we unwittingly keep on acting as though we were free in taking on battles that we call our own simply because we have only read about them or seen someone else standing for them. So, let us be against the system. Which system? The multinationals. Which multinationals? As far as I am concerned, I think that the most important and powerful multinational is myself; as a person, as a man, and as a human being. This is why the weapon of Love is not to be used against anyone or anything. It is to be used to guide people along the path of awareness in total ignorance of the Big Deception which is created inside us and which is nourished by the attention we pay to what is outside of ourselves.

I apologise if the readers of this book expected to find suitable training logs or diet sheets for those who cross the desert, or even enchanting tales told at night while sitting around a fire in the company of Bedouins under a starry sky.

To their surprise, the readers will find out that it is a book about *the desert*.

It is a moment of meditation and expectations. What happened to the supporters of the epoch-making 2012 event? Where are they? Are they waiting for another Maya calendar? So many people expected 2012 to be an international turning point, whereas, as facts have proved it, they could have momentously been able to gradually create a small cataclysm to change their own world, day by day, by using simple gestures and thoughts. If you want to make changes, you should do so and there is no excuse for not making them. Your attempt will however be hindered by having obstacles put in your way, by planting the seed of doubt in you, and by tempting you with seemingly more gratifying, but inhuman, ways.

Nothing will stop me and I will continue growing.

I do not give way to hatred, grudge or delusion which only consume energy and space that deserve to be used differently, mainly in the improvement of one's personality, neither do I intend to influence other people's thoughts and convictions that often make us have a blurry vision of our dreams and goals.

There have been times in my life when I had to sink right down in order to get a strong enough push to make me rise and fly again. In those times, I sought the power of awareness and not of thoughts nor hostility.

It may sound absurd, but the great darkness which envelopes this historic period is making it easier for us to find our way, because lights, even the tiniest ones, can be easily noticed in the dark. The greater the intensity of the dark, the easier it becomes to see light without delusion. These tiny points of light have already begun to gather and are creating a guiding light. There are many small guiding lights, scattered around the world, which are able to attract other small lights that were lonely, helpless, and misunderstood as well. Unity of strength and awareness creates power. Awareness protects people from being blackmailed. This is what my records are about: to make use of the instrument in my hands, the desert, and employ it in a message of awareness of all forms of personal potential.

On the last day of December 2009, I covered 150 km in Sinai in 24 hours, on part of the biblical prophetic path where the waters were divided, up to the monastery of Saint Catherin at the foot of Mount Sinai. I retraced Moses' steps in his exodus to rescue his people and ideally guide conscience to another shape of awareness, which I believe, to be extremely important, namely, the genomic test. The analysis of our genes opens the path to prevention and to targeted and customised treatment which match what is written in our dna. This decreases the possibility of being slaves to a special form of thought which is typically pharmacological in front of "diseases".

Prophets and Messengers of awareness have always been painted in the past as poor men wearing rags, often misunderstood, unshaven, destined to live a life of sufferance and hardship, and obliged to beg. Little, if any, is known about their private mysterious life, let alone their relationships with women, wives, mothers and friends. I would imagine, however, a modern prophet to be potentially in each one of us and to be primarily a prophet of himself.

The modern prophet is a great communicator and a successful man, with a united family to support him. He is rich, very rich actually, because he is honoured for his commitment in passing on experience and awareness. In my opinion, the essential thing lies in a person's character, in his inner quality to do good. It is no coincidence that the oldest proverbs show how money is a great soul detector, being able to amplify resources and weaknesses in human beings. It is highly probable that if a poor man with a wretched and hostile heart won 100 million euro, he would become wealthy, but perhaps he would be even meaner and more arrogant than before, and would use his money the way his soul would lead him to. On the other hand, a poor, good-hearted man, given the same amount of money, would very probably be generous and spend his life using his fortune in helping others, creating profits for noble purposes, so gaining more profits to share with others.

Using our imagination, a so-called "mystic person" might conjure up an image of someone who hides in a cave, is always fasting, who is misunderstood by the outside world and is always willing to cherish the Truth as he sees it. However, I believe that a modern mystic person, whether sitting in that cave or in his own flat, could just as easily be found updating his Facebook/Instagram profile, spending his evenings with his family and helping his children with their homework.

The revolution is in seeing ourselves as potential wise prophets, understanding what we want to say and trying to spread our word, through art, work, our appearance, or any other field of our lives.

If Prophet Jesus (PBUH) were to come back (and it is said that he is already here), he would be very upset about how his name has unrestrainedly been merchandised to make profit. Before throwing the merchants, who still exist today, out of the temple, he would chase away other merchants from other places of worship where people sanctify money, war and as many other gods and goddesses as human injustices.

It is the same Jesus whose pictures are on the walls of our houses and in whose name someone of us has been baptised. The very same Jesus who we often forget all about on Christmas day, because we are too busy unwrapping presents or arguing at the supermarket cash register that very Christmas Eve. We are convinced that a church mass can wash our conscience clean after a whole year of hypocrisy. Actually, it matters very little whether Jesus was really born on Christmas day or eight years earlier or later, or if 25th December was the ancient pagan festival of Sol Invictus. What is important is what that day really represents and not what had really happened back then.

I strongly believe in the symbolic meaning of Christmas as an occasion which can help us reflect on the emotional aspects of our life; in the surprised eyes of children; in the charm of the snow and homemade pastries; and in the family gathering around the table which is an occasion that, unfortunately, has become increasingly difficult to make happen nowadays. I do not believe in pretence, imposed actions, the futile stress of unwrapping presents, the multiple messages sent to contacts listed in the phone directory, nor do I believe in wasting time and money on social pretences. Ah, I do not even believe in Santa Claus dolls hanging on the walls of houses. But this is purely a matter of taste.

My path in life, not just in the field of sports, has sometimes been laden with difficulties, like when I was in Pakistan, Afghanistan, Yemen, Palestine and the Holy Land, where I found a machine-gun pointed right at me.

I arrived at the West Bank, and was supposed to run from Ramallah at Mount Sinai, passing through Jerusalem and the

Gaza Strip. I witnessed, first-hand, the two opposing and specular points of view between the Israeli and Palestinian worlds. These views are reflected in a seemingly bigger world, that is, the Arab and Western worlds. I personally met the Palestinian President Abu Mazen and I spoke to those who have to live a life which we only read about or watch on television: the people of Gaza, Ramallah, Jerusalem, and Tel Aviv.

I came to the conclusion that most people know very little about the historic and cultural background of the Middle East issue. Therefore, the only information, coming from Western media, is biased and incomplete.

However, we make our opinions, points of view, beliefs and actions on the basis of the scant information in newspapers and on television. We then use these opinions and points of view as a topic of conversation in our day to day lives. This creates a gap between people from different cultures and geographic origins. It creates misunderstanding at the expense of knowledge and cultural enrichment.

In those journeys I also discovered a new unprejudiced perception of reality and information.

All I aim to do is observe, elaborate and share information about my experiences with as many people as possible. All of this is in the name of a deep and unconditional understanding of the origins which create attitudes that we somehow define as correct, depending on our origin. I came to realise that history does not actually teach anything: Afghanistan, Pakistan, Yemen, Iraq, the Middle East in general, are represented by media as the evil to be eradicated, while the Western world, which has killed nearly 100 million native Americans (Red Indians), is depicted as a saving force (though it is not clear from which danger they will save you).

 On the other hand, right from childhood, we are accustomed to the idea of shooting Indians and, oddly enough, the evil to annihilate is always beyond our own reality, even in the Middle East.

History is restricted to "the Day of Remembrance". On that day we must summon up our memories and try to remember all the victims. Dear politicians try to remember all the victims who deserve to be remembered: the American black slaves and their descendants; the millions of Chinese and Russians killed during communist revolutions; the millions of Armenians slaughtered by the Turks; the Tibetans exterminated by the Chinese; the inhabitants of Hamburg and Dresden as well as those of Hiroshima and Nagasaki; the genocide of the Cambodians; the Australian aborigines; the Kurds, the Chechens and the people of Bosnia and Kosovo. Must I go on? Yes, missions of peace were held hiding under war weapons. I say this as a man who has worn a uniform and won the military Pentathlon, and not as a pacifist who has participated in a street march. The industry of love and peace gives more profit than that of war. I confirm this, and my idea is based upon studies by people who are more experienced than me. The arms industry can be reconverted. It is a long way to walk, but it is not impossible.

This does not mean abolishing the military machine, but handling it in a different way, as a deterrent and not solely as a tool for economic interests.

Of course, my desert is not made only of sand dunes. The whole world will become a desert if we do not steer towards the direction of deep awareness right away. On a global level, this could be solved with fair harmony of resources, races and souls.

The world will not change unless *we* all change, and this could happen if we decondition our minds from external influences and start to consciously filter only what we want to seep into our minds.

My signature, analysed by a psycho-graphologist, shows that nothing is impossible, once I have made up my mind. I accept all challenges, even that of emptying the sea with a teaspoon, should that challenge be necessary to save even one single soul. I would do my best and I would invoke divine help to stand by me in the mission. Maybe a change of gravity would empty the sea or a meteor would pass close to earth and make the sea evaporate. I would in all cases be there, holding my teaspoon and my strong belief.

My force.

The Force Within.

ORIGINS
WHERE WE ARE BORN IN OF LITTLE MATTER:
WHAT COUNTS IS BEING BORN

I look back and see a lot of passion in everything I have done. That very same passion which makes sacrifice and suffering seem normal when there is a dream to fulfil.

Nowadays nobody wants to suffer, and sacrifice has become a memory linked to our ancestors and past generations. I remember a sad experience in Niger: I can still see the image of a girl who was destined to die because of a small injury to her knee which was infected to the point that her leg developed gangrene. The wound had been treated by the girl's parents with water taken from a well which animals used to drink from. Some basic treatment, which is low-cost by our standards, and better hygiene could have saved that child's life. What we may take for granted (a simple injury) can turn into a tragedy in another society. I left that hut in the middle of the desert in anguish and with a wrath in my heart.

Today we throw away millions of packages of medicine in the bin because they were left to expire and become unusable, while that girl died because she did not have a single box at her disposal. I thought about all the medicines I have at home: they are unused, wasted, destined to be thrown away in the bin or are out of date.

There are children who struggle to survive while others have everything, even impossible things. It is anything but sacrifice! I am sure that sufferance moulds us just like metal is shaped in the hands of a blacksmith. It is only then afterwards that we deserve to have the latest videogames out on the market. There are rules, tracks, models in which we can direct our efforts and those of our children. Certainly, sport in general is a great help. If you get up at 5 am on a Sunday morning and go for a healthy walk on the mountains, you will certainly do things in moderation the night before.

If a training session in the swimming pool is needed to make you fit for your race, you will certainly not smoke a whole packet of cigarettes a day. We spontaneously adopt these rules, rather than impose them on ourselves.

As an athlete, I come from a mountainous area where alpine skiing and extreme climbing were hard workouts and daily routine. I started skiing at the age of six, though I also took up other sports as pastimes such as windsurfing, volleyball, water skiing and judo. Yet, I always longed to be in touch with nature. I wanted to be free to run naked with my body touching the grass in the meadows, the flowers and tree bark. I wanted to breathe the crisp air of the mountains, not only through my nostrils, but also through every pore in my skin. At the age of ten, I took part in a Sunday non-competitive run of only 10 kilometres in my hometown, Portogruaro (a small town in the province of Venice-Italy). The time it took me to reach the finish line was so short that everybody thought I had taken a short-cut.

I had not taken a short-cut though. I had simply used all my potential, and had even amazed myself at the speed and intensity of my effort. When I arrived home, I began to suffer from severe chills and a blurred perception of what surrounded me. I felt like I was about to collapse, but said nothing to my mother. I think that was the first time in life when I risked to die as a cause of over-exertion.

How many aspirations have we had as children! "When I grow up I will be an astronaut, a doctor, a pilot…" Each one of us has had a dream. As soon as I saw them, I was enthralled by the images in an encyclopaedia about Saudi Arabia and the countries of the Arabian Gulf. The book was titled 'One Thousand Searches'. My mother had bought it at the old Pellico cinema. I clearly remember that afternoon when so many families in my town gathered for the presentation of that brand new, trailblazing encyclopaedia.

My mother wore her best clothes and I sat next to her, hoping she would decide to buy that book which, to my eyes, represented the answer to all the doubts I had about my relatively small world. I also hoped that the small instalments proposed by the chubby convincing seller, would allure her into buying the book. My wish came true and my mother signed the promissory notes after only a moment's hesitation. I gave the chubby man a hand to put those heavy volumes into our blue car, a Fiat 127, feeling like the richest child in the world.

Once home, we arranged the encyclopaedia volumes one by one on a big chest in the hall. My mother did not really care much about whether the books were closed in a cabinet or put on display. She just wanted the books to be in a suitable place for my height so I could pick one in the same way delicious strawberries might have been put on display to be grabbed and tasted. I remember being immediately drawn to the volume that had an orange cover. It was about geography of the Middle East. Leafing through the book, I read that there was a "Pirate Coast" in the Arabian Gulf, which is the nowadays United Arab Emirates and Dubai. I also found many other curious facts which

I felt like I had already learnt about. In the chapter about Saudi Arabia, I was drawn to one photo in particular which showed a caravan crossing the border of Rub Al Khali desert which was described as "absolute emptiness" and "nothingness". A Bedouin sitting on a camel.

I was completely captivated by that photo. I mentally plunged into it and saw myself, a grown-up man, walking alone between the very high dunes on a cold, starry night. I took my crayons and drew a picture. It was 1974 and I was 7 years old.

The picture represented the Arabian desert as I had imagined it, without even having seen it before: a large blotch, deep red in colour, which covered the sheet of paper. I was not influenced by anything when I drew the picture because, even if it included part of Egypt, I did not draw the Canal of Suez as is the case in all maps.

I wrote '2010' in the corner of it. I took it to my mother and said "Mother, when I'm old, in 2010, I will be the first man in the world to cross the Rub Al-Khali desert." My dream was to search inside our world for a place that was still unknown, not necessarily on the moon or in space, just a place where no man had ever trodden, be it a desert or his inner self. In 2010 I did not try to run the great desert because life prevented me from making my dream come true, so I decided to postpone it in order to face a challenge called 'routine' first.

I was fascinated by everything that was unknown. "Why", I wondered, "has no man ever been able to get into that desert? Why did the Bedouins and their camels dread it, only daring to walk along the edge of it?" This has always fascinated me tremendously.

I was impressed by the man on the moon, precisely because he was the first man to set foot where no other human had ever been before. His eyes saw what no other living being had ever been able to see before. If there are now doubts about man's landing onto the moon and about whether that landing was real or a hoax, it does not really matter to me.

What matters is not being able to do what no one else is able to do, but to think about accomplishing something that no human being has even dared to think about and which would be deemed "impossible" once revealed to the world.

Maybe someone else will accomplish this in a thousand years' time, but you will have been the first to have rendered that mission possible. If I remember correctly, it was Einstein who said that some things may seem impossible until a person who has no idea about them is able to achieve them. I would add that you need to rid yourself of all prejudices, all previous experiences and face anew without thinking about how you might have approached it before now. Nothing is the same as the day before, and even if it were so, it is you, man, who changes.

This was my dream. My innate curiosity and thirst for knowledge. A desire to give an answer to every 'why'. As a child, I liked to pose many questions to myself so I could explore and discover the answer myself. Today many adults do not ponder upon the reason for so many things and life goes without having been given a real meaning, or without at least an attempt to do so. If we do construct this meaning ourselves, it is often for fear of realising that we are all alone. We were born naked, but we spend a lifetime covering ourselves to the point that we look in the mirror and do not recognise our very selves anymore.

Where are our childhood dreams?

"You wanted to be an astronaut, didn't you?"

"Well, I could not study, then I got married and had two children, then..."

These are all excuses. You have lost the match with yourself. It does not matter if you haven't become an astronaut. What matters is whether you still hold on to the conviction that you could have become an astronaut and that you would still be able to if you wanted. A dream cannot die if the force inside you is strong enough to keep it, though, unfortunately, it may often lie asleep and appeased.

It seems easier to give up than to fight and suffer a lifetime to make your dreams come true. I'm often asked "Why go to all the trouble?"

I would be tempted to answer "What about you? What makes you the way you are? Are you perhaps dissatisfied with your life, in a job which does not fulfil your needs, but which you will never leave for fear of change? Are you in a relationship to a woman or a man you don't love?"

Giving up is often easier than fighting. I have always decided to fight for my dreams to the end of my days. I draw happiness from trying, daring and never giving up. This is how I feel rewarded, regardless of whether my dreams come true or not. Each one of us should do this.

Therefore, I will answer to the question "Why go to all the trouble?" by asking you "Are you happy?"

ASPIRING EXTREME ATHLETE
EASIER SAID THAN DONE

Crossing the desert all by yourself is a challenge that does not need only a physical approach. It is quite obvious that the physical preparation required is of the highest levels in order to be able to face and tolerate extreme fatigue and pain. The workout has to go beyond all physiological boundaries studied so far in the controlled and doped world of sport as well as show business and must overcome the barrier which, being physical, imposes a limit from the onset.

What I mean is that if I have to run a 42 kilometers road marathon, I train to a workout and diet regime based on previous experiences and analysed from medical, sports, biomechanical and nutritional perspectives. I also have to wear special kinds of shoes and clothes. At a given distance, I have to take supplements like maltodextrin and energy bars. I try to adhere to certain running speeds and have a regular cadenced pace during each kilometre I run. At high levels, things change drastically. The athletic action is pushed to maximum levels to reach certain points within unimaginable time limit thanks to new discoveries in the field of medicine and science.

Now, picture doing this in an extreme setting. In sports, for instance, an athlete can run one kilometre in 4 minutes. Keeping the same pace, the athlete is able to cover 42 kilometers in only 2 hours and 48 minutes. If the athlete then carries a 10 kg backpack and tries to cover the same distance, he realises that his speed decreases and he needs 5 or 6 minutes to run one kilometer. 42 kilometers at a lower speed will now take him 3 hours and 30 minutes to complete.

If the athlete is then given a 15 kg backpack and is asked to run on mountain creek stones, his speed reduces further and ends up needing 7 or even 10 minutes to run a kilometer. Running on ground that is not only stony, but also flat for having been smoothed by water is very dangerous because of the risk of ankle and knee injuries. Imagine, then, running in a rocky desert, carrying a 10-15 kg backpack on your shoulders. Each step is like a hammer blow to the ankles, knees, and back. In Oman, while I was crossing the imaginary line of the Tropic of Cancer, I had to cover a distance of 437 kilometers, about 270 kilometres of which consisted of hard, chiselled and sharp stones.

Now, in this simulation, the aspiring extreme athlete will have two more "basic" elements to deal with: sand and nightfall. Have you been to a lido in summer? Imagine yourself comfortably lying level with the first row of parasols on the beach, or even better, sitting near the water's edge. At a certain point, let's say at about 2pm, you begin feeling thirsty and hungry. The heat is unbearable and the only desire you have is to get a cold shower. You leave your deck chair and walk the 100 meters between you and the longed-for kiosk, passing by the rows of parasols and sun-loungers. Your stride will be heavier because of the sultry weather and the clammy sweat on your body. Your feet sink into the scorching sand so you try to seek shelter immediately in the shade of a parasols to keep your feet from burning for a while.

The worst thing comes when you reach the last row of parasols. A neutral area is between you and the kiosk. There isn't a single parasol in sight, nor even a signpost to provide shade. There are still 30 meters left before you can reach the kiosk. I repeat, 30 meters. Those who are brave would try walking without looking for a shady spot, but after few arrogant steps, made pretending that the heat could be stood, they start running on their tiptoes, keeping their wallet in their hand until they reach the finish line: the beach kiosk.

Now imagine you are back at the last row of parasols watching the horizon. There are just sand dunes, but no kiosk. The kiosk is 200 kilometers away and not 30 meters from the place you are standing. The parasols are not there anymore. There is sand everywhere, behind you, in front of you, under you; everywhere. And the sun is beaming down on you. The weather is so hot that it is unimaginable.

I will try to give you an idea of what that is. On a very hot August day, your car is left all day in a paved parking area with its windows closed. There is no trace of shade anywhere. You are about 5 kilometers away from your car, wearing heavy winter clothes for running, including a pure woollen hat and pair of gloves. Remember that you are dressed like this in the month of August. Then you wait until it is 1 pm and you start running on the sand to reach your car, carrying a 12 kg backpack. Let me say it again 'there are only 5 kilometers to go'.

When you arrive at the car-park, you find your car parked in the sunshine, while you are sweating all over. Sweat drops dripping from your forehead inevitably slip into your eyes making them burn. You instinctively wipe your eyes with your hand, but you hand is sweaty too and your eyes burn even more and you find it hard to see. Now you open your car door and immediately get in. It is suffocating in there! Help! You want to get out to get some fresh air. You try to take you clothes off but they are glued to your skin. Your head bubbles. You are about to have a nervous breakdown. Enough! Now start your car and turn the heating up. Leave the windows closed. You would reach the point of wanting to scream for some fresh air. Your head begins to boil. It is not over, not yet. Now imagine that you ask a person who is close to you at that moment, to press the palms of his hands onto your temples. You tell them to stop as it begins to hurt, but they do not stop and carry on pressing for hours until sunset, forcing you to scream. Then, what about water? When you find it, it is hot, just like the water in the bottle you have left on your car dashboard under the sun.

This is exactly how you feel when you are alone and helpless, facing extreme conditions in the desert in the scorching summer.

If you multiply these 5 kilometers by 70, you will get the same conditions which I faced in the desert of Oman in the middle of summer. Those sands hide so many dangers. If you want to watch a live episode of National Geographic, just give me a call and I will take you to a natural set with its real protagonists: scorpions, snakes, lizards, green lizards, desert foxes, hyenas, desert leopards, camels, goats and an infinite number of poisonous and non-poisonous insects.

Then night falls and you have to use your senses to do as best you can. A moonless night is so dark that you wonder whether you'll see the light again or not. When the moon is full, you wonder why it is not as shiny in our countries. In any case, if anything falls to the ground, whether it is a moonlit night or not, you have to be very careful of the "hosts" I mentioned above, which obviously become very dangerous when disturbed.

At this point, after coping with sand and nightfall, this aspiring 'extreme' marathoner who wants to run the Tropic of Cancer in Oman shall be given some 'assurances' and we can imagine a dialogue with him.

"My dear friend, no cars drive in the place you are treading. So, there is no doctor to help you during your run. This is the rule."

"Heavens! This means that if I misplace my foot and sprain it so badly that I can't walk, I won't be able to reach a doctor. So, I have to be extremely careful with each step I take."

"Of course! You'll have to be careful with every step. If each pace takes you ahead by an average of 80 cm (on sand or rocks), the 437 kilometres you are going to cover will need about 500,000 steps on the ground, therefore you will have to be 500,000 times more careful!"

"Ok, everything is quite clear. If the worst comes to the worst, I will use the satellite to make a phone call so you will come and pick me up!"

"You don't have a satellite phone and you cannot call anybody! Besides that, nobody will know exactly know where you are. The only thing we are able to go by is that you need to reach a precise point where we have access to because there is a track or a trail there, maybe. That point, however, might even be 120 kilometres away. We won't be able to get to the place you are by car, simply because the road is not accessible to cars, nor quads. We won't even know where you will be at that moment in time."

"Oh, but I thought that... Oh well, call for help if you see I don't arrive!"

"Yes, of course, but that won't be any earlier than 48 hours from your scheduled arrival time, simply because that is the agreed-upon waiting time. Only then will I try calling for help, but who do I call? The police, of course, who will answer in Arabic or in English, if you are lucky! And what should I say?:

'A friend of mine got lost, send a helicopter!' 'Where?'

'In the desert of course!'

'Yes, but where exactly in the desert?'

'In the desert, near the mountains of the Tropic of Cancer! Remember that high mountain?'

'Yes, after the sand dunes there is a stony plain then there is a mountain.'

'Yes, but where exactly is the person who is supposed to be lost?'

'What kind of question are you asking! He's down there of course, in the middle of the sand. I guess! I don't know where he is now. Maybe he is already out of the sands... Listen, I am not quite sure!'"

"But, isn't there any support by the local authorities of the country where you are running, may be by using a helicopter or a satellite detection system perhaps?"

"Of course there is support. It's me. Here I am! I have a lot of excellent connections. I have so many mobile phone numbers of Ministers and Emirs, but if you want to become a real extreme traveller at least once in your life, a free spirit, without an alibi, then these are the rules"

"So?"

"So, you have to know that if something happens to you..."

"What?!"

"Nothing!"

THE DIFFERENCE
SAME CLOTHES, DIFFERENT PERSON

Many competitions are masked by extreme feats, but do not represent anything such thing in essence. It is just like reading about someone who has single-handedly crossed the harshest deserts, only to discover later on that he had a pace car following him, a tent ready to be set to give him shelter, and someone at a few meters distance ready to come to his rescue when necessary. Incomplete media information puts the final touches to the picture: "Incredible! An extreme athlete has crossed the desert of ..... in just 2 days and 3 hours' time." or "It is the first time that a man (or woman) has ever crossed the desert of ..... on foot." This kind of news makes me smile. Why does it not tell the truth? The walk took 6 days and not 2! These six days included eight hours of sleep a day and periods of rest, which leaves only 2 hours walking time. I once read "A historic feat: a 350 kilometre of single-handed walk in the desert of ..... in only fifteen days!" I immediately thought that there must have been a misprint. 350 kilometres in 15 days? This means 23 km a day! I'll say it again: 23 km per day, with a follow-up guide ready to pitch a tent when needed. With all due respect, anyone could have covered 23 km per day for 15 days or even less than that with the assistance of a guide to follow and help him prepare meals. The walker omitted to say that a jeep occasionally passed by with tourists on board who held out bottles of beer or, even worse, some motorcycles and quads passed by at full speed on the dunes or on the walking route.

Such information is incorrect, and readers have the right to read the truth. How can you speak about the silence of the desert and the will to explore and find oneself if, deep down, you fear being alone with yourself? How can you speak about the silence of the desert if you are constantly followed by a car with a running engine? A journalist should report correct information, to be read by the protagonist or his team first of all and then by the readers who can then make a judgement for themselves.

Any person who breaks these "records" will not lose any of his emotional or human aspects, because each one speaks about and conveys first-person experiences which reflect the real meaning of being adventurous which can be made public through true, undistorted information.

There are excellent and real extreme athletes in the world. I feel a very fine thread uniting us when I speak to them, which is something profound and quite unexplainable. I think it runs in our DNA.

What I wrote about extreme experiences reported by journalists or by those who claim to have lived it first-hand, metaphorically reflects what happens in daily life in which we are often "forced" to believe that the news coming through the media is true, as we are forced to convince ourselves that we have specific desires, simply because those desires are unreal and have been created.

In the long run, any relationship (writer-reader, interviewer-interviewee, artist-audience or husband-wife, for example) based on a lie will end up turning into a black stain which can be very difficult to erase. Having to remember all the lies been told, the people who the lies have been told to and act accordingly, is a enormous source of stress. It is better to tell the plain, unvarnished truth. Yet, things take the opposite direction. This often happens and in almost any source of information: politics, news as well as romance.

When watching the national news bulletin, have you ever wondered "Why are only these specific pieces of news reported amongst all the events taking place in the world?" Who filters and chooses the news for us? On what basis do news bulletins tell us about a show-girl's latest love story, yet not say a word about a massacre in a remote village in the Sudan or about the killing of children bought and murdered by immoral paedophiles in Southeast Asia? Given this, why should foreign newspapers give a more trustworthy idea of what is happening in my country of origin, Italy, for instance?"

On the same day, we can buy the Herald Tribune, Le Figaro, Al Quds, Gulf News, the Washington Post, El Pais (to name but a few) and a national Italian newspaper. We leaf through these newspapers, page by page, until we reach the international news and important events happening abroad which all the world must know.

Despite the importance of this news, sometimes Italian newspapers dedicate full pages in the "foreign news section" to gossip columns at the expense of more important political news. At the same time, foreign newspapers publish headlines and articles about issues we which we have no idea about in Italy, but which we should absolutely know about. North Korea and its nuclear arsenal in the hands of a madman; genetic modification of food crops (GMO) and its imminent presence in our foodstuffs without us being aware of it; Indian universities providing high-profile engineering graduates who are widely sought after and can speak perfect English, while in Italy we waste our time enhancing dialects; Zimbabwe and the conflict in Somalia (an issue that was only ever mentioned in Italy when

Italian soldiers were involved in missions over there); a genocide in a small African country at the hands of fundamentalists (not only Islamists) who looted villages, raped women and children and then killed them with machetes; and finally, there is the conflict in Sri Lanka, Congo, Burma, and Chechenya.

I would like to ask you now if you could tell me where the countries I mentioned are geographically located (though I admit that I would find this difficult, too) and why these countries' issues were so important that they deserved a whole article to be written about them in the newspapers or television programmes, yet were instead replaced with other articles dealing with our national politicians' debates?

It is difficult to give an answer, but the concept is simple: ignoring a problem is like confirming that it does not exist. On the other hand, bringing a problem to light means calling upon governments, institutions, international communities to take responsibility. We ourselves, sometimes do not take responsibility for even trivial things just because we refuse to be responsible. We talk about vaccinating 40% of the world population against the latest flu virus and we forget to say that two million people are dying of tuberculosis. Do you know how this will end? It will end up in us getting up in the morning only to hear news bulletins talking about the usual summer crime (names change, but not the essence of the story), the sad ending of a love story between a business magnate a show-girl who suddenly has become an actress, singer, show-host, dancer, and minister, and the difficulties she had faced until she was able to overcome moments of great distress. People will listen to all of this and be completely fooled. This will become normality.

At the same time, "good" news comes through the mailbox, tucked in between the dozens of advertising leaflets: "*starting this month, home-related expenses such as bills and fluctuating mortgages will increase by 100 euro a month, simply because the town hall has decided to increase property tax as well as the cost of recycled waste*" as well as "*since you have not paid your car parking fine it has now doubled in addition to added expenses*, but you can submit your appeal to the Justice of the Peace if you want."

Then you go to work, enter a coffee bar, order a coffee, encounter a friend and start talking:

"Hi, How are? Everything OK?"

"Oh, yes, everything's OK. And you?"

"Everything is fine. Thanks."

"Have you had a coffee?"

"No. It's on me!"

"No, no. Let me pay for it."

"So, let me order. One black coffee and another with a dash of frothed milk, please."

"Did you watch the news bulletin yesterday?"

"Yes! What's your opinion?"

"I have always thought that it was the mother who killed her son, even when I saw the interview with her neighbours."

"No, I do not think so! I think the killer is one of the town inhabitants, but he cannot be prosecuted for lack of evidence."

And so the conversation goes on...

"It's been very hot recently, hasn't it?"

"Oh yes, we can no longer distinguish the four seasons, can we?"

"OK, I have to go or I'll be late. Say hello to your family. Bye!"

"Bye!"

This cliché is often repeated during the day.

We get a feeling of satisfaction when we are talking to other people, even if we are not communicating anything at all. Families who still have the good habit of gathering around the dinner table, have to deal with the problem of television and smartphones invading their mealtimes which would not let you listen if one of your loved ones – your child, your wife or husband- spoke to you. There is so much indifference. The average time dedicated to family dinner is 13 minutes. The dining table is set:

"Come on, dinner is ready!"

"Daddy, do you know that today at school..."

"Excuse me, my mobile is ringing. Give me a second."

Answering the call:

"Hello! How are you. No bother at all(!)..."

Returning to his child:

"So, what were you saying? Oh, yes! School. What did you want to say?"

"Today something happened at school."

"Hold on! Keep quiet for a moment, please. Turn the sound up on the TV immediately. Just take a look at that! What a terrible accident on the motorway! All because of the fog!"

"Ok, go on now, tell me what happened at school."

"Dad, today at school ... Sorry dad, I have to text a friend of mine."

"Can you pass me some water, please?"

"Let's just be quite for a while. You can tell me what happened at school later on. People have been talking to me all day and I just want to relax. We'll talk later on, ok? Maybe after the game show, or after the special programme about... or maybe later on."

Do you think I am exaggerating a little? Of course I am, but only in the description of the situation, not in its substance.

We no longer listen to our children, our parents, or our grandparents. How can I possibly think of crossing the desert and hear it if I am not even able to listen to myself?

The desert is not just sand. It is also the way we conduct our daily life while trying to overcome the pitfalls of our social life, other people's interference that rocks our boat and harsh thoughts as well as other things. We have reached a point at which we know everything about a TV show host or about our sports idol. We know what they eat, what their hobbies are, their love stories, and even how much they weigh, but we have no idea what size our child's feet are or which class they are in.

We do not even know who we are. Do you realise that we do not even look at ourselves properly in the mirror? We try hard to remove a hair from our nose or set our eye brows, but we do not realise that the small mole we have on our shoulder has become as big as a lentil. It is other people who make us notice it. Why didn't we notice it despite looking at ourselves in the mirror daily for years. Why then should we criticise what we see in others if we do not even see ourselves?

Why should we see the Middle East as hostile when we only look at the desert and at the Arab World? The concept of the war in Iraq and Afghanistan is different if seen from the point of view of a Muslim country. When I read the Gulf Times or Al Quds, and when I watch the Arabic channels Al-Jazeera, Al-Arabiya, the BBC and CNN, I realise that things are portrayed differently to how they are in our TV programmes and newspapers. This means that there are different ways to see the same thing.

Many still believe that Arabs apply the law of retaliation and that women, all women, wear the Burqa. We think that in Iraq there is nothing but weapon attacks and that all the people are all trapped in their houses, while foreigners are beheaded in the suburbs. Why do we forget that during the times of colonialism, it was the Spanish, Italians and today's Europeans who committed the worst crimes, chopping off the Arabs' heads to display them as trophies or killing defenceless women and children as well?

Baghdad is a city where people work, go to university, read newspapers, go to the gym and where women go to beauticians as well as being a place where 5-star hotels are inaugurated. In brief, it is a city where people lead a normal daily life. Of course, there is a very delicate political situation, the concept of which is not very much different from the Bologna railway station massacre nor that of Capaci (Sicily) massacre, for instance. I have been frequently asked: "Aren't you afraid of being kidnapped?" When asking such a question, however, how come we don't think about the possibility that a person can be raped at 6 pm in the centre of Rome while parking their car? I would probably be more afraid of walking at daytime in certain neighbourhoods of our Italian cities. I would be more afraid of finding somebody in my house, stealing my things and threatening me with a screwdriver pointed at my throat. I would be more afraid of entering a bank and being involved in a robbery, of going to a pub or a nightclub and finding certain people who, under the well-known effects of alcohol and drugs, try to have fun by disfiguring a person to save him paying a plastic surgeon! We should use our head to reason and understand the real facts before expressing a certain point of view.

Freedom of thought is the only thing left for us, so let's use it. The image given to us about the Arab World is that it is a world full of fighting; kamikaze attacks; struggles between Palestinians and Israelis; clashes between those who want mosques and those who don't; Al-Qaeda and Bin Laden and the likes who are frantic, wearing turbans, holding machine guns and shouting slogans against infidel dogs; the Taliban and everything else that comes to mind and that I have forgotten to add to this black list. We are even afraid of anything written in Arabic or of a Muslim who is praying. This fear is based on ignorance. Yet, we are not afraid of Arab money, nor of the fortune we make by doing business with the Middle East.

Now I will deliberately try to provoke your feelings. The ex-manager of a national Italian newspaper who publicly converted from Islam into Christianity in front of eight hundred people during the national book festival in north-east Italy, claimed that *"the Quran verses legitimise an ideology of hatred and killing [...] I am convinced of the incompatibility between Islam and the values for which I have always fought"*. Everyone applauded.

I will not comment and I will not say if what was stated is right or wrong and I will not reply either, because freedom of expression is one of the foundations of democracy. However, I wonder how many people among those eight hundred people actually have an idea about Islam, Judaism, and the Bible. I would also wonder how many of them have since raised a barrier between the two cultures after having listened to that speech. They will have raised their wall not because of conviction but out of circumvention, because the audience's awareness about the religious aspects which govern the world, are mostly based on taking a quick look at some newspapers or watching snippets of news bulletins or documentaries which speak about the Muslim world.

Meanwhile, the way of collective thinking is oriented towards a rift and increased hostility between the two worlds. So much for Christian compassion!: *"You shall love your neighbour as yourself." In spite of all that, our way of thinking is still conditioned. "Who knows what they will say? Maybe they are getting ready for an attack... Look what he is doing! He is kneeling and praying to Allah. Their God is different from ours."* How come the two Gods are different? One thing that is different here is the *prejudice* behind it all. You judge those who pray to God! Yes, ladies and gentlemen, *they do pray!* They pray to God, just like all Muslims who pray five times a day do. One God, the God of Moses and Jesus. Muslims begin praying and reciting the Quran from childhood, and this is their power and strength that the Western world has lost. This is compensated with kids cursing as they walk around smoking cigarettes and with a European Union that is based on divisions rather unions, despite its name. Let me tell you something: people, guided by ignorance, are still talking about issues they do not have an idea about.

Let me ask you a question: do you know anything about the Jewish Torah? Do you know who wrote it and what it says? Have you studied the Quran and do you know who wrote it? If not, how could you even dare to think about using the religious aspect to criticise Muslims and defend the Jewish? Why does it annoy you to know that Muslims do not eat pork despite all the delicious ham and sausages we have in Western Countries , yet you do not criticise the Jewish who do not eat pork either and even use different cutlery for different kinds of food? Why?

Maybe you have never been to an Arab country or the Holy Land neither. I assure you will not get to know an Arab country simply by spending a week's holiday in a resort on the Red Sea.

Let me ask you another question. Have you ever read the Bible? You haven't? Oh, dear children, you have received the three sacraments of Baptism, Holy Communion and Confirmation and even got married in church! So, how come you do not know the origin of your actions? If this is so, I had better not ask you the name of the evangelists, then. Let me repeat my questions: who wrote the Bible? Can you tell me what the ten commandments are? What is the Book of Deuteronomy? You will be greatly shocked to know that the Quran dedicates a whole chapter (surah) to Mary, mother of Jesus, and that the Quran recognises Jesus' ability to perform miracles and says that Jesus will be there on the Day of Judgement. For your knowledge, Jesus and his mother and all the prophets are mentioned in the Quran which might shock you to know. Your astonishment and scepticism will increase to discover that Moses is also mentioned in the Quran. Didn't you know that all God's Messengers were sent to their people basically to prove the oneness of God? The Quran considers Mary to be above all women and she and her son were immune from Satan's touch. Now, try to think for yourself. Do Muslims really hate the Jewish and want to eradicate them from the face of earth? How can they not love Jesus and Moses who are more Jewish than the Jewish themselves? It would sound like claiming to hate all "dirty negroes", yet love the black president of the United States. Try to give it some thought because the information we have about Islam and the rest of the world is not a hundred percent true. Think about this huge contradiction in another light: you hate all children, while you love your 5 year old child at the same time.

There are other people to mention: the atheists, the Satanists, the disciples of other religions and cultures, and those who are believers without a religion, including the extraterrestrials. Islam will increase its popularity in the Western world, not because of the existence of Al-Qaeda terrorists, but because westerners do not convincingly and strongly spread their values, and because they perform their spiritual practices, first and foremost, for materialistic benefits. Would any of you be able to say the Lord's Prayer in the office before beginning a day's work? Most of you probably don't even remember that prayer, and even if you wanted to pray, your colleagues would be worried about your condition and would advise you to see a good psychologist and to ask for a week's leave. Muslims are Muslims everywhere they are, in Italy, in the US, and even in the far Australia. Believing in Allah (God) is the noble purpose that Muslims share. On the other hand, a Christian is an Italian Christian in Rome, a Latin-American Christian in Argentina and an Indian Christian in India. There is a big difference between two people who meet in a place they do not belong to, who say "I am German and you are Russian", and two others who say to each other "I am a Muslim and You are a Muslim no matter what your origin is. You are a Muslim just like me." Faith is the most powerful link that has ever existed. It creates a togetherness in believing in one God, and respecting, as much as possible, the rules set by the religion that a person has decided to follow. Let us leave each to their religion, and let us remember that people love, not kill, in the name God.

History tells us about the times of Saladin, the Crusades and, more recently in 1893, when a group of Italians were massacred while looking for work in salt mines which were in Camargue in France not in an Arab country. The massacre was named after the area where it took place, Aigues-Mortes. The victims were immigrants from Piedmont, Liguria and Tuscany and they were killed as a consequence of xenophobic prejudice and not for religious purposes. However, had the incident involved Jewish or Muslims, the historic perception would have changed significantly. Since 1998 (as per the Corriere della Sera newspaper), only two articles have been published within its pages in comparison to the 139 references to El Alamein. There would have been thousands of references had the incident been attributed to Muslims and to the French. How many Muslims practise their religion in Italy, then get drunk? Likewise, how many Christians go to church, then steal the same day? A Muslim man covers his wife with the Burqa and rape a woman in miniskirt. A Christian may be working as a volunteer at church but may beat his wife at home. We do not want mosques. If Muslims have their mosques in our country, then we also must have the right to have churches in their country. The real problem does not lie in having mosques or not, but in keeping this division because the more people are divided, the easier it is to manipulate them. A famous saying, dating back centuries, is "*Dividi et imperat*", or in other words, "Divide and Rule".

Not many people know that a church was inaugurated before the summer of 2008 in the Emirate of Qatar. This church, *The Church of our Lady of the Rosary*, had been strongly wanted by a former Capuchin bishop of Arabia who had persistently pushed for it just like other Franciscan Monks in the Holy Land. In any case, churches, just like any other thing, are built if they are really wanted. If you want to build a house, you have to go to the town planning office at the Municipality first, after which, whatever you want to build, be it a church, bridge or dam, you must have the will to do so, since those things cannot be built with words alone. Silence leads to silence. Actions can produce even concrete and bricks.

The Arabs in Europe reflect only part the Arab World, but not that world as a whole. Very often ignorance makes us classify believers in Allah, who decide to relocate to Europe either by their own will or for need, as potential terrorists or as a threat to local culture.

Cultural differences among countries where Islam is the prevailing religion, are not even taken into consideration. There are big differences among North African Muslims in Morocco, Tunisia and Algeria. They, in their turn, are different from Libyan Muslims who are different from Egyptian Muslims, who are different from those of the Arabian Peninsula and from those in Persia, Bangladesh and so on.

We might get very upset if, for instance, a citizen from Dubai told us that we are similar to Croatians, Slovenians, Germans, the Polish or French, simply because we come from neighbouring countries. We usually differentiate those who live in the city centre from those who live in the suburbs, just as we brand those who go to a particular restaurant or public place. We are so highly influenced by the media, that if we take a plane and see a bearded man wearing traditional Arabic clothing and holding a bag with a shoulder strap, we may presume him to be holding a bomb. Let me tell what happened to me when once I took the Eurostar train from Venice to Rome. I usually buy Arabic newspapers which, of course, are written in Arabic and I read them on the train as a way to spend the four hour journey and improve the foreign languages I have learned. I had my seat booked. I was wearing a sweatshirt with Arabic writing on it and was holding the Al Quds newspaper, which is internationally renowned. I sat down and started reading, and I noticed straight away that some people were watching me with furrowed brows. I could see that they were wondering to themselves *"Who knows where he is from? But he is elegantly dressed. Who knows what is written in that newspaper? Why should he choose to sit here and not in another place?"* After about twenty minutes, I left my seat to go to the cafeteria for a coffee, leaving my backpack on my seat. Heavens! Why I did that? I noticed a flash of mistrust and terror in the eyes of the people, as if there was a bomb in that backpack. At that moment, I exclaimed *"Don't worry, I am Italian and from Portogruaro!"* I heard the people give a sigh of relief and mumble something along the lines of *"We apologise, but, you know, it's the stories we hear out and about."*

That's right, I thought. We hear lots of news around. What do you mean by "out and about?" I just want to make it clear that if you say you're Italian in some countries of the world, the word "mafia" would be the first thing to be said to you . I remember that Italians in the past were marked and ridiculed by associating them to spaghetti, pizza, mamma, porno-star at the Parliament (do you remember that blonde who used to play with the boa and then became a member of parliament?).

What can I say about that gloomy period of the Red Brigades; massacres, like that of Bologna; the bomb attacks against Falcone and Borsellino; assaults on armoured cars which ended up in so many killings; corruption as well as people being killed at the hands of the camorra. What a beautiful image Italy has abroad! Fortunately, we have the football world cup championships, so people stop talking about the real problems and focus on how to win matches.

However, I love Italy in spite of everything.

This country is famous for its culture which dates back thousands of years to the times of ancient Rome; for its works of art which are appreciated and visited by millions of tourists every year; the Mediterranean cuisine which is a source of inspiration for great chefs; skills to make dream-like things like Ferrari or Lamborghini come to life; the made-in-Italy fashion worn by men and women of different walks of life as well as the culture and religion of this country. We should not forget that Italians have a gift, even if is often mistaken, for taking life lightly and ironically. This gift, if taken seriously and consciously, can enrich daily life with art and can generate the strength to face difficult moments. I am proud of being Italian and I always enjoy saying that. Whenever and wherever I am, I can always find somebody who wants to be friendly and likes talking about football, pizza, and Formula One.

However, what do these reflections have to do with the deserts I explore? These reflections are more important than the workout I do and the water I drink.

In fact, you cannot cross a desert if you have a preconceived notion about the people, culture, history, and religion of the host country. If you are conditioned by ignorance, you cannot judge and disapprove of other people's actions and feel at rest when you are alone with them in the same place, that is, the desert which gave birth to the Arab world, and in a country which has been once famous for its legendary stories of the Arabian Nights though is now apparently no more than a factory producing

48

Islamist terrorism, according to western prejudice.

Your situation would be a contradiction, just like a politician who inveighs against Islam but has never read anything about the Quran, or a person who is for or against the Palestinian issue but does not even know where the Gaza Strip is and thinks that Fatah is a lady with a magic wand in her hand, not knowing that it is a political organisation. We are ready to flaunt the rights of women "forced" to wear the veil, and ready to condemn indistinctively. However, we forget that in very small towns in Italy, not so long ago, widows were obliged to wear black scarves on their heads and black mourning clothes. This custom can still be seen in the same towns in the South of Italy where women had to "save themselves" for marriage and would display blood-stained (or tomato-stained) bed sheets to boast about lost virginity. These are the same towns where beating women was not a crime. Let us think for example about "crimes of honour" which gave a man the moral right to kill his adulterous wife or her lover, allowing him to leisurely go to the stadium instead of being put in prison. "Crimes of honour" were abolished by law number 42 dated 5 August 1981, one year before the football world cup in Spain. And how many cases of rape have been justified by saying *"She allowed it. She wore a skirt to provoke"*!

What I am getting at is that evil is everywhere on Earth, but we always tend to see it in those who are different from us, as if unconsciously, we refuse to see evil in our homes. Rights denied to human dignity are spread out in the Arab world. At this very moment, in some African countries, some girls are being subjected to stone age rituals of female genital mutilation. Thousands of paedophile western tourists go to Southeast Asia looking for children who are sold for very little money. These children are then forced to face indescribable barbarity and even death. Before talking about the Burqa worn by Arab women, let us speak about Nepal where, apart from monks, there is much less spiritual issue which needs to be mentioned in order to stop thinking about absolute categories. Each year twelve thousand Nepalese women and girls become sex slaves. We need to open our eyes and know that the stereotyped Santo Domingo, Thailand, and Eastern European Counties are not the only places where human trafficking is practised. The Himalayas are not only a place for mountaineering, but also for sex tourism and trafficking of humans who are sold to western tourists. Very young girls are snatched from poor villages in the north of Nepal and usually sold by their own parents for very little money. A baby-slave can be bought for less than 300 dollars. She then ends up in one of the Nepalese brothels where she is whipped, tortured and beaten up if she ever dares to rebel. Their virginity is worth a few thousand dollars paid for by perverted middle-aged Indian or European men who take pleasure in raping virgins. Because they have been paid for, these girls can be tortured and even killed. These girls do not wear the Burqa. These abuses are the result of inexistent laws, wide-spread corruption as well as lack of censuses of people under 16. In Nepal, girls who usually get married at the age of 13, are subjected to their father's and brother's will until marriage provides her with a husband who she must then blindly obey. This abuse happens under the blessing of an old engraving dating back to 400 AD and kept in a Buddhist monastery near Kathmandu, showing the plea of a woman to be reborn as a man as a reward for her virtuous deeds.

Should we also talk about North Korea, or about depriving

thousands of people of their right to honest jobs and obliging them to pay "hush money", which sometimes means usury and other times leads to the suicide of the payers? There are innumerable examples, yet they are all united by a single thing, that is, they all have an origin. Babies are born innocent and pure, but their behaviour begins to change under the influence of external factors beginning with their search for breast milk and concluding in their relations with other people.

It is precisely in those moments that a person decides which path to take: the good or the evil. So the question to ask is not what can be done to stop an Arab terrorist or a paedophile because it is too late, but rather what can be done to allow newborns to choose the path of goodness when they reach the age of decision making? The "human" system here faces a very deep problem, and man starts to look for technical solutions, laws and other methods which are largely doomed to fail.

DANGERS IN THE DESERT
MORE PEOPLE DIE ON MOTORWAYS THAN IN THE DESERT

I would like to start by saying that, geographically speaking, deserts existed before the birth of man. They were inhabited by living beings whether animals, plants or even spiritual entities.

This means that a madman running alone in the desert could be considered as an intruder who can disturb the harmony of the environment which must be then defended. On the contrary, in the case that that man is sane, it is he who needs to be defended. The same thing happens when we walk on the numbered footpaths which are set by the Italian Alpine Club and which have been used by thousands of people climbing up the Dolomite mountains.

The dangers are the same but the protagonists are different. A mountain viper wouldn't bite you because it wants to eat you (you are too big a prey for it to swallow), but because, for some unknown reason, you have jeopardised its safety. You might have sat down on a stone under which the viper was hiding and trampled on it by mistake. The same thing happens in the desert. One day in Mauritania, a snake crawled under my back in the dead of the night. It was cold (about 4 degrees) and dry, and the snake was seeking a warm and humid place to stay (my back). I did not realise it was there immediately, but I did feel something moving, but believing it to be just a mouse, I did not worry too much. The only thing I was thinking about was my sacred 7 minute micro-cycle of sleep and that nothing would have prevented me from enjoying that siesta. Then, I sat up and shone a light on the stone which I had been lying on. To my surprise I saw that divine creature coiled up, as if it were asking me to lie back down again because we had been cosy together there.

Of course it is not so nice to find yourself face to face with a cobra hissing at you from in between the rocks of the Oman mountains, nor is it enjoyable to spot a leopard in the distance in the desert of Yemen. This animal is similar to a big cat and when you see it, you feel like calling it with "Hey dear, come here!", but if it starts staring at you, you realise that "Dear" is very hungry and you must find an escape before you end up having your calves torn to pieces in its jaws.

Of course, before sitting down on the ground, I always move the stones and the sand and check all holes that may lead to borrows under the dry bushes. The shape of the burrow and trails left by animals are clues to what type of creature is in the shelter.

Yes, "*creature*" that's what I meant! Why should only cats or dogs have the privilege of being treated like humans in our homes, while a poisonous scorpion in the sands cannot have the privilege of being my friend?

You might reply "It is because dogs are man's best friend. They are intelligent, affectionate, faithful and even seem to be talking to you sometimes."

Tell me why, then, do the Chinese eat them?

It's all a matter of relativity.

Can you imagine how powerful a desert scorpion is? I could crush it under my feet if I wanted to or let it crawl on my hands and face without even being afraid. Am I crazy? No, I am not as crazy as those who keep a pit bull terrier in their houses, tying it up with a 30 cm chain, which would make the dog so stressed and angry that it explodes at the first time it is stroked by a child who mistakes the dog for a fluffy toy.

Scorpions are the kings of the desert and I consider them sacred. I would also like to give an insight into the other inhabitants of the desert stones and sands I met on my treks: the oryx which is similar to a gazelle and has long and straight horns; the tahr which is like a cross between a sheep and a chamois and has small backward horns; some rare species of hyena and jackal; the arabian fox which is similar to a normal fox but with sand-dray fur; the fennec fox with big ears that the animal uses to radiate body heat; the Arabian leopard which is very shy and bashful and of which very few examples are left; the wild cat also known as the lynx; the mongoose; the hedgehog; the porcupine; the desert kangaroo rat which is very similar to a small kangaroo in the way it stands on its hind legs and which is considered as delicacy by the Bedouins who cook it by splitting it in half and cooking it skin-side-down directly on fire because its skin is so tough that it acts as a shielding pot; different kinds of fast-running big lizards; various types of poisonous and harmless snakes like the sand cobra, which comes to welcome you once it notices your presence, besides many more.

Even camels can be dangerous, though not so much for their character as for their size. It happened to me once, that I literally bumped into a camel in the middle of the night, although without any serious consequence because, fortunately, I collided with the side of its belly. Had it been with its face, I could have fractured mine. An interesting thing related to camels is that in extreme situations when the Tuareg cross the desert, they may kill a camel to quench their thirst by simply cutting its hump and drinking its contents of blood and water. The amazing thing is that the Bedouins do not catch any disease caused by bacteria or microbes by doing this, because they also make use of the leaves of a plant which has a highly bactericidal effect.

In the end, man is and will be the real danger. Don't you think that our world is becoming too arid and sterile? Now, we, single individuals, are surrounded by a so-called "scorched earth". We are there alone and ready to be killed at the first misstep and for futile reasons. The worrying thing is that we could be killed not only for serious matters, but also for unexpected, trivial reasons. An unpaid telephone bill is like receiving a reminder by a lawyer saying 'If you do not pay in three days' time, you will face death!' Yes, death! A death threat does not necessarily mean you will be killed if you don't pay. It means you become so obsessed with this issue that you begin thinking about it day and night. You begin to wonder why it happened to you, an honest and a hard-working person. When you bought your house, you had your salary to pay the mortgage. You are now unable to pay because your company has closed down and you have not been paid yet by your suppliers. The only time that it happened that you were late paying a bill or mortgage instalment, you were treated like the worst delinquent on earth. You may see on TV that in some countries, those who steal, kill, rape, or use drugs, not only are not put in prison, but also become famous by dint of interviews and publicity, not to mention the large number of corrupt politicians who enjoy numerous benefits in defiance of the law and honest citizens. Exasperated citizens might say "So, I can steal as well!", though we know where that would lead. If a hungry person stole an apple at the supermarket, he would have an immediate and fast trial without the possibility of having any leniency.

So, tell me where the real danger is.

TRAINING
DO YOUR UTMOST, THE BEST YOU ARE ABLE TO DO,
ALWAYS AND EVERYWHERE

I am often asked how and how long I train in preparation for an extreme challenge; how, to what extent and in what way I can combine my training and my family and social life. Any answer would be misleading because the question itself is not in line with my way of thinking.

Let us think about how many workouts we do and what kind of training we need to do to get ready for work, marriage, a trip, or even an important interview. We have often heard professionals in a certain field of work claiming that they do their work more out of passion rather than duty. This is why they never count how many hours they work a day. They say that even if they became wealthy, they would never leave their job for another one that required less hours' work from them if it made them feel less satisfied. I feel the same way about what I do even though it is in a different dimension.

I would like to affirm that I have never trained in my life!

Thinking about training and working-out would violate my personality and what I want to do. I have never thought about training by running alone at night in the woods and in the dark in the rain, nor have I thought about sleeping on well-arranged stones in my terrace, just to get my body used to it for the desert. I would do it, though. Thinking about training means that I would be "forced" to do something and achieve another. However, I know that I would behave the same way even if I did not have a challenge to face, and I will always try to seek out those situations that help me feel good and liberate myself from my body through physical sufferance that reaches the point of annihilation so that at that very moment of being without a physical burden, I can push myself beyond the boundaries of my mind.

I have frequently asked myself how I could train to face the life I was leading and not only to explore the desert. There was an itinerary in which there were so many common points where running on the soft sand was like sweating blood to work in the midst of snakes called competition, unscrupulous colleagues and false friends. I have willingly chosen not to train and I have always worked for the pleasure of it, achieving very rewarding results. Crossing the desert or having a certain amount of money were not the goal, but the consequence of what I do.

We can achieve a significant goal if we do something, whatever it is, without expecting anything from it: acting for the sake of it, acting without constraints, acting without any set reason and letting our unconscious guide us instead. In this way we are reacting as free people.

One way to gauge how much you identify with this line of thinking would be to ask "*Would you continue working if you won 140 million euro at the lotto?*". If your answer is "NO", then your job is something imposed on you.

Some might consider investing part of this amount to start a business in their field of expertise because they love their work so much that they can give work opportunities to others and can continue doing something they have always loved and believed in. Who knows if a person with 140 million euro in their pocket would still want to keep their wife (or husband or girlfriend or boyfriend) and walk together towards their future life. Some might quickly fly to a desert island; others would migrate to another country; while others may radically change their social life or their friends to have a more stimulating life; some might even decide to free themselves from all bonds chaining them to a woman or man who they could not leave for economic reasons or for fear of being judged by their families.

It is obvious that sometimes we come face to face with hypocrisy about our presence on earth and I mean the harmful choice of having to spend all our life pretending to be what we are not.

It is like the difference between training and unconscious natural needs. It is the difference of the actions we might do with or without winning the lottery. We should, however, try not to do the things we would not do after having won the lottery and we should not use those things as a short-term strategy to reach what we most desire and what best represents us. We should move towards improving and enriching our real situation and satisfy our unconscious needs. Many times we feel the urge to change but we don't do it and try to convince ourselves that it is just a question of money. Money is important and fundamental, it helps us eat, raise our children and finance our projects, but it is much weaker than our dreams. It is a consequence of being listened to with discipline, not an aspect to chase. A dream is so powerful that it can never be stopped by anyone or anything. We can reach our desire some way or another. In the past I made personal choices which brought about economically difficult moments. However, I have never thought about giving up my dreams and explorations for even a single day. I could have changed my job to solve my difficult situation and emerge from those dark times. I never gave thought to such things though, thanks to my ideas about the concept of poverty and wealth.

Had I been the poorest or the richest person in the world, I would still risk my life in the desert. I would even go further. Every day I try to push my explorations further, in order to find answers to so many mysteries about inaccessible places. Since I am following my dream and my heart, I am sure I will find the answers about my life and if this happens the answers will always be clear.

Let us begin to distinguish the things we are obliged to do from those we want to do because they belong to us and we would do them anyway.

Do we really want to waste our life sitting in front of the television? Are we sure that that armchair is in front of the small screen simply because we want it to be there? Perhaps we consider this a necessity because we are unconsciously conditioned. A lot of children are shoved in front of the bright, colourful television so that their parent can have a moment to relax with some peace and quiet. How much more often would it be important to have someone close, and be hugged by their mother or father?

Unfortunately, words like "Switch on the TV and watch cartoons so we can relax for a moment!" are not unreal. That moment becomes hours, days, months, and years. Those cartoons replace parents to the extent that the child begins to refuse those parents that he has always loved, because their presence would disturb him while watching his superheroes. It is an incredible sight to see a parent be shooed away by a child who wants to watch a cartoon. When the child grows up he will remain influenced by this false need and believe that his freedom is represented by sitting on that armchair every day, including Sunday afternoon. He would say "You know, I do this because I want to and not because I am obliged to."

This is exactly what I mean when I say that we have to distinguish between what we are obliged to do and we really like to do. This is real workout! It is a real mental training because it allows our bodies to follow the direction of our instinctive desires elaborated by our logical thoughts.

Of course, you will have to work hard, suffer and perhaps even cry and scream in pain, but in the end you will be able to choose the place which allows you to feel free. Having said this, I will now tell you how I get ready for an extreme challenge.

It is very difficult to describe, because everyone measures things according to their own experience. If I say I run 400 km non-stop, this distance might be perceived by others as inconceivable or incomparable to their own experiences.

Extreme free climbing and ski mountaineering have shaped me physically and mentally. However, they belong to surroundings which I have always felt as restricting because they did not allow me freedom of expression. I have often found the mountain to be small and limited. I turned my head and all I could see were houses, cars, other people, buildings and animals, besides other things. I always longed for the extreme, without limits and alone. Completely alone. Without an alibi. Without emergency services within reach. I have always wanted to reach absolute extremeness and do something greatly significant that no other person has ever done before. It is not a matter of showing off, but because I do think that man is able to go beyond all unthinkable limits.

I have never believed in the way of tackling problems by starting from the easiest upwards. I have always thought that the earlier you have to deal with severe hardship, the more likely it is that you avoid years of successive minor difficulties.

The same logic can be applied to desert exploration. In 2001 I started participating in 'extreme desert competitions' which were considered the toughest in the world. I wanted to participate in all of them, but I soon realised that the 2,500 euro registration fee in 'this' or 'that organisation' was the only extreme thing I had to face. I was nothing but a bib number amongst others. The run was in the desert, but what kind of desert was it? A desert with a car in front of and behind us and a helicopter above. There were also tents and doctors always on hand to treat even minor problems, like a simple blister, for example. We could also call home, our girlfriend, wife, office and others, and there was a computer that we could use in the evening to chat or write to a journalist friend who could write about us in the local newspaper as if we were real heroes. In that kind of situation, you would not even make out that the girl next to you has never run in her whole life, and would not realise who the person talking about animal extinction and dressed like a rhino is.

I thought "Dear paid-for bib number, look around you! There in the desert, there are shepherds and Bedouins who can use the food you have in your backpack to eat for a whole month! You complain about a simple blister while there are people in Africa and who knows where else, who have never worn shoes and whose feet have toughened so much that a nail would bend if you try to fix it there."

So, what is the question here? What is extreme for one person, might be everyday life for another. Each one of us has their limit which must be reached and overcome thereon. It does not matter if this happens at Central Park in New York or on Jumeirah Beach in Dubai.

The aim of an obese or sedentary person to run 10 km non-stop is equivalent to my extreme challenge of running 400 kilometres non-stop in the desert. I would rather say that the former challenge is relatively more extreme than mine. On the other hand, I would absolutely consider the 400 kilometre non-stop run to be a absolute extreme action because going beyond the limit is to reach the point of no return.

People create satisfaction and esteem for themselves by setting a limit to reach or shift. It is however necessary to dispel some urban myths such as having to drink one's own urine to survive in the desert, which is a ridiculous notion and against all medical principles. Imagine that while you are running on the scorching sands, you run out of water and continue sweating of course. Then you feel the need to urinate. It is logical that without drinking water and having continued to sweat, you will not produce three litres of clear urine, but maybe just a bit more than half a glass of highly concentrated, nauseatingly smelling urine, which will burn your mouth the moment you try to drink it because of the high concentration of urea in it. However, imagine that you drank it. The consequence will be that you will not urinate any more if you are dehydrated, your body will consume the small amount of water remaining within the muscle fibre to dilute the salts you have swallowed. You will continue to sweat and you will be increasingly dehydrated to the extent that the kidneys will begin to shrink and a kidney transplant will be your only solution then.

There are so many realities to be told in order to describe what the desert really is, what it is like and, mostly importantly, where it can really be found.

It is almost impossible to compare a desert exploration with any other kind of competitions through technical or distance terms or by comparing it with the effort and heat sustained in any other standard competition. In a desert exploration a person has to be ready for the greatest human sacrifice that might end their existence in this world,; that is, the sacrifice of one's life which could be at risk in a extreme desert exploration.

Having said that, I will now tell you the secrets about my training; I, 'the man of the desert'. Night-time and sleep deprivation are the most difficult things I face during desert explorations. Therefore, managing sleep deprivation is the first aspect to deal with. The second aspect is suffering which can be faced solely with mental and spiritual training, without using any medication. The last aspect to deal with are hallucinations, which are due to extreme effort and which can alter one's perception of reality and put one's life in danger even in commonplace situations.

Everything else, like running shoes, food or GPS are not a priority and are insignificant, actually, compared to the above priorities and it is easy to explain why. I could be wearing the best shoes ever and have the best GPS, but if I am having hallucinations in the middle of the night and do not realise that I am walking towards a sand depression, the so-called "quicksand", my 200 euro shoes will surely not be able to save me because what type of running shoes I am wearing does not make any difference at all in such a situation. I am often asked about the type of shoes I wear and my answer is that when I train I sometimes wear a brand X size 46 shoe on my left foot and a brand Y size 44 shoe on my right and vice versa. Nothing should be taken for granted. If someone told me they have tried different shoe brands but are still suffering from pain in their foot arch, I would suggest they change their foot, rather than the shoes, which isn't impossible to do.

Choosing running shoe types is important for a race on paved ground, a mountain dirt road or in the mountains, because different shoes are needed according to the ground you tread on. The best shoes to wear in the desert are those that feel like you do not have them on and which leave enough space for your toes to be comfortable and your feet well aired, even if you keep them on all along the 450 kilometre run on sand and stones and in hot weather and a temperature of 50 degrees. Next time you buy shoes, I would advise you to try on different brands in the dark without looking at which brand is which.

 Take a look at the brand only after having chosen the shoes that fit you best, and you will be surprised at your choice. I have made my choice, challenge after challenge, because my feet choose different shoes and they are almost never the same. This happens because we are very much conditioned by how something looks and this happens with everything, not only when we choose shoes. We could say a bar of hazelnut chocolate is delicious, eating it in the dark, but we might not feel like even tasting it if we see that it looks like human excrement when the light is on.

It is a preconceived notion because we are conditioned by what we see and make our judgement accordingly. This situation is true when we are making a judgement of items like shoes and their advertisements or of people. If someone advised me to eat one type of food, rather than another, I would ask *them* to eat the food they recommend me to have. There is no fixed rule and the touchstone is what our body needs, once it has been purified from mental prejudice. I will never eat energy bars, not only because of the heat and the difficulty in preserving them, but also because of their sweet taste which, in extremely dry weather, would make me nauseated and physically sick. On the other hand, I go crazy for grated coconut, walnuts, almonds, peanuts, dried meat, powdered milk, very salty vegetable soup, and I may have some crackers or dry biscuits. Basically, if we consider that the amount of energy needed is 100, then 90% must come from fats and proteins, while the remaining 10% must come from complex carbohydrates. Standard pasta is not included in that diet, nor are coffee and dried fruit, with the exception of dates and figs. I have a little secret though: I always drink camel milk before I begin my challenges and I keep some of this milk with me for the first 24-48 hours, simply because this milk does not easily deteriorate even when it is exposed to the sun. My diet does not include sweets nor food supplements. The only thing I concede myself is a cappuccino made with soluble barley coffee, which, like all the food I take with me, can be found at any supermarket.

I nibble very little amounts of food and sip water constantly. I am inspired by the mystic Sufis' way of thinking in regulating my diet and sleep; that is, to eat as much as a sick person would and sleep as a castaway would. I, and I alone, decide what to eat and how long to sleep. External inspiration must always be shaped and tailored to suit us.

Excessive food and sleep render me lazy and make me waste time. In the desert this is a rule followed by all its inhabitants and is not a forced law, and in this way people are not slaves to anyone. Lastly, I would like to say what I think of water. Water reliability and purity certainly depends on its composition, the dissolved solids in it, and the source it comes from. What is more important, though, are the features of the person who offers you the water. You have to smell the water before drinking it. Water as it is, does not only contain sodium which goes to all parts of our body, starting from the stomach, but also the energy that water has after having flown long kilometres through soils, rocks, sediments and culverts. Therefore, let us invert our way of thinking at least once and try to drink air and breathe water instead.

In conclusion, I do not depend on sports medicine in choosing how to train and what to eat, but rather on what my body and instinct, guided by my brain, require in a specific moment. Besides this, it would not be possible to standardise diet and use the same food elements in extreme and normal environments. There are too many variables, the first of which is each and everyone's personality.

SUFFERING
WHY SHOULD WE CAUSE SUFFERING TO OTHERS IF WE DO NOT ENDURE IT OURSELVES?

We are not used to suffering and making sacrifices anymore. There is a specific medicine for each kind of pain. There are different medicines for headaches, the flu, a cold and so on, or maybe they are all the same medicines, but with different names. We use medicine to chemically ease the pain because it is an obstacle that prevents us from getting on with our tasks. However, things should go the other way round. If I sprain my foot, pain becomes the instrument for me to understand that the problem cannot be solved if I walk on my foot. In this case, pain protects the injured part because it reminds us of the problem each time we put our foot on the ground. What can be done if you are walking in the middle of the desert and have an unlocalised, but widespread pain in your body? Taking too many medicines would not solve much because no medicine has been experimented in such extreme conditions and for so many long hours. Besides, I am against using chemical substances that can alter the perfect equilibrium of my body. On the other hand, how can it be that the same dose of medicine, let's say a 10 mg tablet, would have the same effect on billions of people?
I have always thought that a standard dose is actually the minimum efficient amount of medicine that provokes the fewest side effects possible to provide benefit (which is sometimes questionable). The ideal dose is the one that does not solve the problem but alleviates the disease and has minimum side effects. In this way, the medicine can be sold to

millions and millions of patients who find it beneficial and who will buy it once again.

Obviously, I am not speaking about serious diseases and pathologies for which medicine and research have succeeded in finding definite cures, providing improvement and a better quality of life which might have been unimaginable a few decades ago. Unfortunately, some pathologies require taking certain medicines for life.

What I am talking about is our general attitude in the case of those illnesses which are attributable to affluence; those which we do not try to tackle with changes in our eating habits or lifestyle, but by relying on medicines to solve the problem instead. When we suffer from back pain, for example, the first thing we do is to take pain killers or anti-inflammatory medicines, instead of trying to improve our posture, do some physical exercise and change our diet. In another example, some types of diabetes patients are treated with insulin which allows them to eat those foods that can increase blood sugar levels, rather than prescribing them a specific diet that controls the level of blood sugar. The last example is of patients suffering from high blood pressure caused by stress, caffeine, smoking and eating salty food, who prefer to take medicine so they can continue leading stressful lives.

I think that the best solution lies in finding the right combination between a lifestyle that suits our bodies and sparing the use of medicines until the problem has been solved as far as possible. I would first try solving a physical problem by following very strict and rigid dietary, physical and mental rules in which medicine would sustain me but would not replace my energy.

Some of the medicines on sale are more effective thanks to the placebo effect which increases the effectiveness of the active ingredient. If we want to cure our headache with a medicine, unaware that it is made only of sugar, it is possible that the headache would cease all the same. This says a lot about the power of what we believe in and its effect on our health.

Our health is the most important thing in our life, but we have become a large easily-manipulated mass with predictable behaviour. We have now the absurd belief that pregnancy, which is the most natural and spontaneous aspect of life and which has allowed species to continue, is an illness.

Nowadays, a pregnant woman is considered like an ill person is. This makes us believe that Mother Nature (a pregnant woman) is sick, too. It was the only natural image that had remained pure and untouched; nothing more than waiting in reverent silence for the magic moment of childbirth to welcome the new creature to the world. Nowawdays, if a woman says she is pregnant she is told "Do this! Do that! Don't do this or that! Take this or that! Attend prenatal and post-natal classes! Attend anti-depression post partum classes! Wear maternity shoes! Eat food that is suitable for pregnant women! Watch films that are suitable for pregnant women! Have an epidural childbirth!" and so forth.

So, the terrorised future mother spends nine months with terrible doubts that can only be confirmed or dismissed by a doctor and tests she undergoes so she can be told, in almost absolute certainty, whether or not the unborn baby is suffering from an illness or malformation that everybody thinks about, but never talks about. It is precisely that term "almost absolute certainty" that eats up our mind and thoughts.

In this way, a hospital is considered a reality on which a woman's health is based. The obstetrics and gynaecology departments are part of a hospital, hence the name *department*, and this is where a pregnant woman gives birth and is examined by doctors.

A hospital is a place where sick people are treated, and a pregnant woman is part of this group. She is examined by a medical professional who wears a white coat, the thing that unconsciously evokes the idea of illness. The consequence is that her stay in hospital will not only be a source of joy for the arrival of the newborn, but blemished by worry about possible illnesses or malformation.

Right from childhood, we are brainwashed even about food and the fact that snacks and other products could inevitably make us prone to diseases for which, of course, there is a remedy. Snacks are made in such a way as to attract the consumers and make them buy more, which is very normal since it is part of legal marketing and is foreseen by the market and its laws, besides being the ultimate aim of economic interest.

Let us then try to free ourselves from the snare of being made to believe that an eight-year old child is better off eating snacks instead of a piece of dry bread and dates in order to grow well. Let us free ourselves from being made to believe that a soda drink is better that fresh orange or blueberry juice. Parents should stop poisoning their children with junk food and saying that it is the child's choice.

Very often we choose our food on the basis of tastes imposed on us in our childhoods, rather than on the basis of our real physiological necessity related to needs of the cells produced by our DNA. We alter the natural attitudes of a child and build an artificial substitute world around him. In many countries, gardens, meadows and trees are removed and replaced by dirty slides and benches covered with filthy cans and syringes.

There are *'NO PLAYING HERE'* signs in the only accessible parks. Since children have to play and grow healthy, their parents register them in gyms, let's say, on Tuesday and Thursday from 6.00 to 7.30 pm. In that gym they roll around on a mat just as they would do in the grass and use the gym tools which replace the trees that have been chopped down in order to build useless constructions or fee-parking areas.

As we see, nature is often replaced by artificial things at the expense of children's physical, creative and individual needs that natural elements can greatly stimulate.

SLEEP DEPRIVATION
WHEN SLEEP IS NOT NEEDED, IT BECOMES A WASTE OF TIME

"There is no god except Him. Neither slumber overtakes him nor sleep" (II, 255).

This text is written in the Throne verse of the Quran. Sleep deprivation is the most testing situation a human being can ever face.

A person can do without food and drink, can stand whipping or being torn to pieces, but nothing can be compared to the suffering of being deprived of a long sleep. A person begins to have hallucinations if deprived of a long sleep, and begins to imagine things that we may see in the best horror films. In short, sleep deprivation leads to losing one's mind.

Fortunately, I can choose how to manage my sleep and am able to stay awake during a single-handed challenge. This means I can move quicker and carry less food, water and equipment with me. At standard speed, it would take me 8 to 10 days to cross a 250 kilometre desert which is usually crossed by Bedouins at a speed of 20-30 kilometre per day on camel back. On the other hand, without sleeping and at a fast pace, I may be able to cross that same unexplored desert, where no cars can get to, in 48 hours, regardless of the type of land. Obviously, this means that my backpack is lighter since I do not need to carry as many things as those needed to run for 8-10 days.

I do not need a tent because I can sleep anywhere on the ground, after having carefully chosen the place, of course. I do not need a gas stove nor pasta with tomatoes. All I need is 2000 calories daily even if my body can burn up to 10,000 calories during a desert run.

Therefore, it is certainly more convenient to run non-stop. Besides, I am less exposed to dangers related to the presence of animals or other things if I lie on the ground for only 7 minutes every 3 or 4 hours. I would not even dare to imagine how many and what kinds of snakes, scorpions, spiders, mice, foxes, lizards, goats, and camels might have passed by, or even over, me during my short naps. During the 30 km exploration of the Tropic of Cancer in Oman near the Emirates' border, I once lay down on my side for my usual micro-cycle nap, but when I opened my eyes, I had to remain motionless as a white poisonous scorpion was about 15 centimetres from my nose and moving towards my mouth, perhaps attracted by my breath. On another occasion, in Qatar, it was night and I felt something breathing above my ear. When it touched me, I could feel it was wet, so it might have been the nose of an Arabian Fox. In both cases, I just turned over and continued sleeping. I only have a 7 minute sleep and I do not want it to be interrupted for any reason whatsoever. My awakening from the micro-cycle nap is immediate and I soon jump back to my feet to set off running again.

The advantage of this is that my muscles, joints and ligaments remain warm and do not suffer from muscular friction which happens due to excessively long pauses. You might have noticed this, too, if you take a break while doing the housework, only to find it difficult to resume your work, simply because the muscles have cooled down.

Scientifically speaking, all I do is have a primordial sleep, which is similar to the naps babies take in their mother's womb whenever they feel the need to. This is called polyphasic sleep. I have developed a method in which I eat little but often without including carbohydrates in my diet to avoid glycaemia peaks. I have short but frequent naps (micro-cycles), according my physiological needs related to an unconscious sleeping and waking pattern which improves my performance.

After birth, and as we grow, we become biphasic sleepers. That is, we split our sleep into two different cycles between night and the afternoon. This also happens to children at nursery school where they usually have a nap after lunch. Then, as adults, we become monophasic sleepers, that is we sleep once a day, except in the cases of professional needs.

I have taken part in some sleep studies held at the University of San Diego (California) and at the University of Udine where I undertook a forty-hour sleep deprivation during training test. In short, I am able to sleep easily in any place, no matter how uncomfortable it is (with the light on, in the dark, with noise around me and I can sleep whether lying on stones or a comfortable mattress). When perfectly rested, it takes me 80 seconds to fall sleep, but when I am under physical stress and sleep deprivation, the above time reduces to 5 seconds. I can sleep up to three minutes while walking in a straight line, even on stones, and I spontaneously wake up according to my mentally pre-planned time, which is usually 7 minutes.

Sleep can be controlled, and over the years, I have created a method that can be customised and used by everybody, even in daily life. This method can help in managing demanding workloads, sports or studies.

I personally think that, apart from scientific studies, our actual external environment has a great influence on our sleep, which is basically polyphasic, and modifies it so it becomes monophasic. I also believe that if man is left alone in nature, his survival instinct would lead him to adopt micro-cycle sleep during the day. When I am in extreme conditions I naturally adopt the micro-cycle sleep. However, when not in extreme conditions, I sleep for about 3 to 4 consecutive hours and spontaneously adopt the micro-cycle method to sleep the remaining hours. During periods of excessive physical or mental stress, I sleep longer and as long as my body requires.

The body and mind may even require 6 or 8 consecutive hours of sleep. This is a necessary condition to *transfer data* from our short-term memory into our long-term memory.

This is sometimes a problem when I have to focus on numbers, dates, and names at the end of each challenge I face. I might even forget my mother's name when I see her. It a transitory phenomenon, but can put me in very embarrassing situations, like when I forget my pin number while standing in front of the ATM booth or when I have to ask for help to find my car in a parking lot, forgetting that I had left home on foot.

Do you think I am in a bad shape? Not really, especially if we consider that that situation happened after 100 hours of sleep deprivation and after having run 437 kilometres in extreme physical conditions. Some people sleep eight hours and still forget about their wives and children left at the motorway service area.

Our daily life, in which we alternate sleeping and waking, is now subject to rules imposed by the commercial needs of the planet. They are the rules of one big scenario that obliges us to follow a single standard which governs the habits and lifestyles of billions of people. Typically, our day is divided into three sets which are structured to guarantee that we have sufficient independency until we reach retirement age. In most cases, we get squeezed like lemons and drained out in the most beautiful periods of our life.

First set: work. Better explained as eight to ten hours per day for at least five hours per week, including the journey to and fro.

Second set: free time. It is six to eight hours a day of time not dedicated to work that includes waiting in the post office queue.

Third set: sleep: it is the time dedicated to recover enough energy to face the first two sets. This includes watching TV in bed before going to sleep.

Total time: a 24 hours. A whole day long. Saturdays and Sundays cannot always be excluded: forty-eight hours which are sometimes spent not doing happy pastimes but on catching up on things we cannot do on the other days of the week such as shopping, washing the car or doing the housework. I know, I generalise things and trivialise the concept of the codified system which subjects our life to a standard scheme which is impossible to escape from. Of course, social relationships, family, art, sport and an endless number of rewarding opportunities also exist. Yet, we are still very limited in expressing our authentic inclinations, because a fair share of our energy is devoured by a pre-established scenario from the onset.

Very often we feel like spending money and further energy as an outburst from some kind of disappointment caused by work or by our relationships with others. We sometimes even do activities that give us temporary satisfaction without thinking about the need for a drastic change. The money we earn can help us fill the gaps in our souls while we try to fill our bodies with food and our wardrobes with clothes.

Devoting ourselves to our souls and taking care of this aspect will help us become self-aware and will not cost us anything. It is just like holding a kind of a grenade in our hands which we can set off in a specific direction so we can achieve our desires in an unconditioned manner.

In this way, people become aware of their worth and strength and realise that they can improve their quality of life and, indirectly, that of the others around them. In the end, each individual plays a key role in the wider *circus show*. The sole individual acting alone, however, does not count as it is only the collective awareness of billions of people that can give rise to social change.

I have read somewhere that if the billion and a half inhabitants of China jumped all at once, stomping heavily at the same time, they could create a strong earthquake.

We have to reach the point of understanding that we can choose to spend a Sunday afternoon in a shopping centre, leave the street to political rallies held by the same faces, and stop watching reality shows on television, simply because our life is the greatest reality we are living in.

The problem is not in being able to hand out a thousand euro more to those who earn below a certain threshold, nor is it to work less hours and get the same salary. Improving our quality of life and reaching a higher awareness takes time, and the *time* I mean here, is the ability to stop and think while the chaos surrounding us moves far away.

We will never achieve what we want, if we feel unhappy simply because we do not have what we long for. If we focus on material things, we will never understand the satisfaction we can have by using the hidden power in our minds.

If we do not have anything, we sometimes pretend we have more than we actually possess. When we cannot afford to have what another person can, we sometimes hide behind a lie saying "that thing is not important for me", though aspiring to be as well off as a friend or longing for the same car which a person we know has or to go on a dream holiday we saw in some photos.

If we earn 1,500 euro a month working in a factory or in an office and spend 250 euro of it on a car instalment, 500 euro on house rent, 150 on the instalments on a mattress and a set of pans we have bought from a television promotion (because we were enticed by the microwave oven, bicycle and the set of pans that came with the mattress), 50 euro for the home phone and internet bill, 70 euro on computer instalments, 70 euro for the electricity bill, 100 euro for the gas bill (including heating and hot water), 100 euro on clothes, 100 euro on pizza we have at the weekend, 50 euro on coffee and some magazines we buy, 100 euro on tax and unforeseen expenses and 100 euro on furniture, it is obvious that at the end of the month we will be elegantly dressed and have a latest-generation mobile phone, but we will be economically suffocated and gaspingly waiting for next month's pay day to come.

Then, mercilessly, something unexpected happens, such as a variation in the mortgage rate, an increase in the highway toll and season train ticket and an instalment of something we bought under the terms "buy now and pay 6 months later". So we quickly take action and get another loan so we can unite all our expenses in one single instalment to make things easier and all of this because we couldn't keep up with the instalments. In the end, however, we can make it, thanks to the possibility of paying in instalments again. So, we end up paying more money to have more money and in the end we have one single instalment of 500 euro monthly to be paid over *only* 7 years. When we have settled our payments, the goods for which we will have dedicated time and sacrifice, will have been replaced by other more modern models. Thus, we end up paying for things we do not possess anymore and face additional expenses to replace the old things, until we reach self-destruction which is the beginning of a nervous breakdown represented by grouping all the outstanding payments together in a single instalment so we can have a little extra money left over at the end of the month to buy an additional item in small instalments!

The paradox in all of this, is that we might get upset when the price of a cup of coffee rises from 1 euro to 1 euro and 10 cents, while hundreds of euro are taken from our money in the shape of withholdings or hidden price increases without any protest on our part besides the small chat we make about it when talking about the topics the media and newspapers impose on us.

I can apply the mechanism I described to personal energy consumption.

Let me give you this example. If my physical and mental energy is equal to 1500 watts and I consume 500 watts to do my job, 250 to clean the house and queue up at supermarkets, 150 watts when I lose my temper in a traffic jam, 120 watts to gossip about people and get angry because of excessive government taxes imposed on me, 130 watts to remain glued to the television while sending whatsapp messages from my smartphone, I will end up by needing to borrow more energy. From a physical point of view, I may increase coffee and cigarette intake, while from an energy point of view, I might hang around with other people who make me feel good temporarily and who may consume all my remaining energy. I then start to run-up bills in order to recover by energy balance, which may lead to the above mentioned expenses. The whole thing is about physical and energy situations being closely connected and liberating ourselves from those conditions which are imposed on us is the first step towards freedom.

Blaming our debts on the euro and politics, is just like blaming a sycamore tree for the death of a car driver who crashed into it because he was drunk and driving at 180 km per hour.

Nowadays, we all look the same, dressed in the same way and following aesthetic stereotypes which are imposed on us. If it weren't so, we might even be excluded from any context in which diversity is considered as an unjustified rebellion against unanimity.

This way diversity, even at minimal scale, becomes a shortcoming rather than an asset. When I was at middle school and even at high school, I was ridiculed because I used to wear sweaters made by my mother's loving hands and because my jeans were sub-brands. I was considered as a loner because I did not stay out late on Saturday nights, and because on Sundays I used to go to mountain huts, run in the open air on steep paths, and climb rocks, without a t-shirt on my back, to embrace the sun. As a non-conformist, I have always thought that certain activities, including entertainment which does not fit in with human nature, should be banned as long as people are actually unable to independently choose for themselves or when there is no other alternative. Contrary to this, our choices will be imposed and not desired. This lack of alternatives is well reflected on the years of youth which is the most beautiful period of life and in which values, characters, and expectations are in positive expansion. Those are the years in which interferences that prevent us from communicating and sharing ideas must be reduced to an absolute minimum. It is in those years that a person is shaped and moulded and in which they eventually make decisions about their future. I even disagree with school imposition which becomes an instrument of "torture" when students are obliged to sit down for hours and hours, instead of following their natural inclination to express themselves, move, shout and run.

Ever since we are children, we get used to sitting still for 8 hours a day when, as if to prepare us beforehand for the 8 hours of daily work that we will have to do for at least 40 years of our existence. We are forced and moulded from a very young age. However, human nature is in exact opposition to all of this.

In few years' time, the young people of today will be lawyers who defend drunk drivers who have run a child over, doctors who tell us what foods we have to eat to keep healthy or politicians who we will vote for to improve our society. Just like most of us, these young people, may have been conditioned by stereotypes that were imposed on them and not chosen by them right from childhood. When they are asked to decide what is good for others, they would do that from the "no other alternative" point of view which I mentioned earlier.

I stated at the beginning that sleep deprivation is the most testing thing a human can face.

Allow me to rephrase that sentence: the most testing thing is to deprive a human from having an alternative when there is a choice, sleep included.

FEELINGS
THE DESERT, LIKE LIFE, IS A COLOURFUL GARDEN WHICH IS FULL OF FLOWERS. WE ONLY NEED TO KNOW HOW TO LOOK AT IT

What is extremeness? It is a very strong, deep and adrenaline-charged theme; the ability to single-handedly redefine limits and recalculate parameters, to start a desert extreme exploration starting with a *forma mentis* beyond all apparent logic. The body is fully controlled by the mind which organises instincts.

I wonder why a person cannot survive in a desert in the middle of summer. To prove the contrary, I go to the desert and walk for 400 kilometres to discover that I can survive this experience simply because I synthesise the everlasting interpretation of the opposites: body and soul. I have a great relationship with the desert in order to not leave the answer, that so many of us are seeking, incomplete. The difficult part of this is in interpreting the message we receive from unexplored places, which are still uncontaminated by past human experiences, because we are used to categorising things in the light of experience. When I run in a desert, which is virgin and pure, it is not categorised according to pre-established notions in mind, but it sets itself free and is available for all those who know how to understand it.

To achieve certain levels of awareness, I had to physically destroy myself, using a method which caused total body exhaustion. I did this to free my mind and give it the power to focus on the needs of primordial instincts. This is in total contrast with the alleged physical dominance in a challenge. The first contradiction is give myself specific limits, because the result will be distorted if I try to find a limit that has been pre-established by a previous experience.

We should not set limits then overcome them, since it is not man who sets these limits, but God, the Universe, and the infinite which, as the word indicates, does not have any limits. Once people rid themselves of their previous experiences to face the desert and life, leaving behind all the sensations their bodies have, the mind is set to wander freely beyond all pre-established limits. If only you knew how huge our untapped potential is.

This explains why I neither define myself as a classic athlete nor as fully introspective. In desert exploration there is no sport at all, but a very profound self contemplation instead. A lot of people attend yoga courses for example, as a way for self-reflection. Just like other meditation methods, yoga is a good instrument. However, I do not practise yoga, simply because I cannot stand being confined in a room with other people, surrounded by smoking incense, I am not able to sit in particular positions and be surrounded by different colours, chakra, stones, thoughts, books, instructors, music playing in the background or say prayers to reach a spiritual path.

I could not force myself to meditate even in front of the sea or on top of a mountain, because at that very moment I would apply an introspection search which is not mine and which is built on other people's previous experiences and pre-established ideas, which do not correspond to my deepest needs.

Various oriental philosophies and many others which have appeared in human lives over the centuries, became divine and were spreading through communication. These philosophies affirmed themselves in specific historic moments and in places where there was reason for them to exist. This is how these philosophies appeared without need for any modification. Everything has changed now, however.

We should free ourselves and shed our skin, rather than engage our mind once again by adding something unknown to us that will tire us even more.

The desert is not just a mystery, it also communicates and talks to us, out of nowhere. In the desert there is no need for incense or music. Likewise, neither is anyone needed to tell us to breathe in and out or to assume a particular posture.

We have to learn how to listen to the talking silence of the desert. Nowadays, we do not even listen to our children, wife, husband, or even worse, we do not listen to those few elderly people remaining who have survived the world wars and lived that historic experience first-hand. On the other hand, we listen to a Zen master who even becomes our spiritual guide. We entrust our soul to a "master" who shows us which way to take, while in fact he should show us nothing because, if he were a *real* master, he should communicate with our soul, but not directly with us, simply by looking at us in the eye and he would not even need to ask us what our name is. We will find our way all by ourselves without the need to a *master*, because it will be indicated to us without need for words. Actually, we do not use our ears to listen to the desert, because it frees us from everything and goes right to our soul, impressing us with the emotions it evokes rather than with images. Each one of us will then learn a lesson to be put into practice according to the needs of their souls.

There is no truth under the sand. However, I seek the truth in it. Legends say that the desert is the origin of everything and is the place where everything began. Legends always have some truth in them because they are created by exaggerations and alterations of real events. Actually, the sand is a metaphorical key that I use to open the door of the absolutely biggest deserts in the world, that is ourselves, through believing, loving and praying.

In moments when I reach the extreme limit, I sometimes wonder "Why do this?" and the answer I get is "Because you can!" We all can, in our everyday life and all of the opportunities and difficulties it brings.

I have never thought about failing and ending up dead and mummified in the dunes, because the positive moment in my heart shall last as long as I can breathe and as long as I can see the sun rise.

There is no particular reason or a precise impetus that tells me that the end is near because everything I have done and will do in my extreme challenges beyond the limits, are just stages along my path. I am just in the stage of preparing myself and everything that happens later on will serve me for the moment I face total mystery which is still unknown to the most powerful satellites that, as we all know, can do everything except taking pictures of the soul. Facing an extreme point of no return is the most exciting, yet contemporarily appalling, earthly and spiritual experience.

The limit beyond which there is something else, is the very moment when the mind is no longer obliged to support a physical situation and is free to expand until it reaches a barrier. First of all, there is still me, but once I am there, I rest my hands on that thing and push further again and again, always moving forward, until I feel a moment of well-being. That moment is so high that I run the risk of not wanting to back up, so for this reason, I have to let it go.

However, a part of myself remains clinging to that barrier which begins to move away. It is only then that I feel indulged in the situation and I return to my body and reality. However, I keep the urge to seek out that something deep down inside; it belongs to me, though I left it somewhere out there and will find it on that barrier when I return the next time.

I recognise that part of me, I recognise myself, I touch that part and try to push it yet forwards. This is why I cannot be anything but the same here as I am over there. This is the reason why I think about man's behaviour, trying to understand how to free ourselves from things imposed on us.

Actually, when I am in the desert, I am all by myself and the only way to survive is to be myself, pure and crystalline just like the grains of sand that make up the desert. There in the desert, it is not possible to be false and dirty then become clean and chaste with the wave of a wand because the desert is merciless. Ten minutes and everything is over. Here is the moment when the meaning of praying and prostrating to God comes clear. The pleasure of discovering and getting closer to the truth is a fully selfish pleasure which I never share with others and never want to share with others. It is a moment of a very intimate joy. I gladly share my experiences and everything I have learnt from the desert with the Bedouins who claim that "God lives there and we have to wake up at dawn at the very moment when the sun rises to see Him."

Man is unique, no matter which race he belongs to, whether Tuareg or any other, whether white, yellow or black. The Bedouins have identified the greatest expression of God in the sunrise which is a moment of victory over darkness and a synonym of energy and infinite power. I believe that God, intended as truth, is there in the night and it is at night that we can get closer to Him because it is easier to see a ray of sunshine in the dark. It is at night that we give a greater cry for help because man, overcome by sleep, is completely helpless spiritually speaking and therefore he becomes an easy prey to negative energy and dark influences. We could wake up in the morning to find our house completely ransacked and emptied during the night by robbers while we were asleep and unaware of anything. Imagine what could happen to our soul at night when we sleep alone in the desert. Someone may try to take our soul away and leave our body lying there. Therefore, it is a matter of faith, not of light and truth.

A proverb in the Bedouin tradition says that it is impossible to climb the mountains of sand to see the horizon, because the end of the horizon can never be seen. I am on the lookout for it. Not the horizon, but the way leading to it. When you climb the sand dunes, all you can see is hundreds of thousands of other sand dunes which are all equal, without an end nor a beginning. Yet, it is impossible to see the horizon, and this impossibility was created on purpose to hide the way. I will confuse you if I cannot convince you to not go there. Those dunes can indicate which way to take only if you free your body completely and let your soul be free. Therefore, those extreme limits are only created by the mind without any initial conditions. The power of the mind prevails over any imaginable physical condition studied so far.

Even if you are the best trained person, you will undermine your certainties and references because they will stop to exit when you are faced with doubt and are all by yourself without a lifeline to hand. It is at that moment that you have no way out.

However, things are not always that well balanced. It might happen sometimes, but not very often, that body, mind and soul are not always aligned. After all, we were born with a perfect mental and physical balance of our own, which is then counter-measured by experience. It is just like having a scale where loads have been put on one of its two plates for so many years.

The solution then is to remove some of the load from the plate and restore balance. It is as simple as that, isn't it?

THE EMPTY QUARTR – AL RUB AL KHALI
THE LAST UNEXPLORED DESERT

The Empty Quarter, or Rub El-Khali in Arabic, is the biggest sand desert in the world. It has a surface equivalent to that of Belgium, France and the Netherlands put together. This desert is uninhabited and uninhabitable. Even oil companies have not been able to explore it fully and the Bedouin do not go beyond its borders. The dunes there can reach 330 meters high, which is as high as the Eiffel Tower. This desert is 1200 kilometres long and 600 kilometres wide.

In 2012, I tried to cross it single-handed in an attempt to challenge the absolute unknown, the legend. Back in 1974, when I was seven years old, I remember seeing a picture in an encyclopaedia taken at the edge of the Rub Al-Khali desert. That picture thrilled me so much that I could feel the warmth of the sun and even the smell of the sand. I also drew a picture of that desert. I believe that nothing happens in life by chance and that our role in this earthly existence is clear when there are unmistakable and strong signals to show us the way. I felt, without any clear reason, that that picture was such a strong sign that I wrote the date of 2010 on the drawing I had done. I showed the drawing to my mother saying "Mother, when your son grows up, he will be the first man in the world to cross this desert where not even camels nor Bedouins dare to tread." I was inspired by the drawing and photo for days as I told myself "Now I know what I want to be when I grow up. I want to know why nobody sets foot on this desert." I felt that I was living a magical moment, as magical as the Rub Al-Khali that I had had in my mind as a child. I had no idea how to be a desert extreme explorer nor what to do to become one. In my dreams and in my thoughts I used to see myself walking and running alone on endless expansions of sand, with a turban on my head to protect myself from the sun. I had a feeling of warmth running through my body, as if I was really in that desert and I pictured I had a tired, sunburned face and strong hands clenching hot grains of sand. It provoked an enormous feeling of happiness. My only desire was to use my soul and all the power I had to make that dream come true.

Despite the promise I made when I wrote the year 2010 on the picture I drew, I could not even attempt that desert, because that year, life brought me a bigger desert to face in my private life.

LEGENDS..
THERE IS ALWAYS A SEED OF TRUTH IN A STORY
NO MATTER HOW IMAGINATIVE IT IS

Do you think that the desert is an uninhabited place? In extreme and single-handed explorations, the word "physical" gives way to "spirit" and "soul", the same soul that makes us all equal in front of the infinite. The soul is submitted to the desert winds which carry answers to so many questions asked in this earthly life.

Legends have a mystic importance which I have to take into consideration when I cross an unexplored desert all by myself.

My Force Within could save me.

Even if this power is in all of us, it is dormant by excessive clothing which covers our bodies. We were born naked to avoid entrapping our soul. There are so many legends about creatures and events that took place over thousands of years in the Rub Al-Khali.

The *Jinn* in Arabic mythology are supernatural spirits under the rank of angels and demons. They are beings of fire or air which are able to assume the shape of humans or animals and can pass through all inanimate things like stones, trees and ruins. They have the same physical needs as humans and can be killed. However, they are free from any physical limitation and cannot be seen by normal humans. The *Jinn* can also take the shape of whirlwinds which are very common phenomena in the Arabian Peninsula. The duty of whirlwind *Jinn* is to prevent people from entering the unexplored area of the Rub Al-Khali. I have seen so many of them there where I heard voices telling me not to enter or cross the imaginary line inhabited by the *Jinn*. If humans harm the *Jinn*, whether intentionally or not, the *Jinn* take delight in punishing those humans. It is said that the *Jinn* are responsible for many diseases and for all sorts of misfortune. However, humans who know the appropriate propitiatory rituals can have the *Jinn* serve them.

I personally believe that it is important to observe where a *Jinn* is heading, because in just a matter of seconds, it could wrap me up and even stop me from breathing by filling my throat with very fine sand, similar to talcum powder, which could even suffocate me.

Believing in the *Jinn* was very common in the Arabian Peninsula at the beginning of its history. The *Jinn* inspired poets and prophets. Prophet Mohammed himself thought that his revelations were the work of the *Jinn*, and chapter 27 (*Surah*) of the Quran is dedicated entirely to them. The legends says that the *Jinn* are powerful creatures that descended from the heavens in the times before the age of Abraham, and this is why they are considered the first rulers of the world. The construction of entire cities is attributed to them and the ruins of these cities still exist in forgotten and inaccessible places like the Rub Al-Khali. Stories say that during the days of King Solomon, the *Jinn* were imprisoned in Sana'a, the capital of Yemen, and that a power blackout pre-announces their presence. There are millions of *Jinn* in the area of Mareb which is within the desert of the Queen of Sheba and gate to the Rub Al-Khali. These *Jinn* are the watchers of that gate and they prevent anyone from entering the desert.

Ifrit are the *Jinn* of hell. Whether male or female, they are all winged creatures with bodies of smoke. They hide in the ruins of the cities in the desert. The *ifrit* can also marry a human being and no weapon or human power can dominate them. However, the *ifrit* can be killed, enslaved, or captured by magic.

Irem Zhat al Imad (Irem of the Pillars) is a city that was built by the *jinn* before the times of Adam. It is said that this city was not built the usual way, with concrete and bricks, like the cities of Rome and New York. It is believed that that city was built using another level of reality which is undetectable by the human eye, and the legend says that that city was built in the area of the Rub Al-Khali. It is said to be the secret gateway to the paths of Supreme Knowledge.

The *jinn* watch over the access to those paths and disorient those who dare to come too close by setting areas of dreams and lack of thinking. The monster of death, sometimes identified as Satan (*Shaitan*) is the absolute and supreme watcher of the Rub Al-Khali. One of the reasons I should sleep at night is because that the legend says that all those who tried to get into the Rub Al-Khali never made it back out again because they fell victims to this entity during their night-time sleep. Maybe they died because of sleep deprivation, dehydration, extreme heat, or as a consequence of their altered perception of reality. I assure you that I have seen all the above mentioned beings, maybe because I was conditioned by what I had read or the tales I had heard about them.

There are endless legends, like the one about evil demons who are believed to be living in this desert. This is why we have to be pure and as unconditioned as possible before taking the risk of going to that place. Some mystic Bedouins suggest that the Rub Al-Khali must be crossed by "non living beings" because the "Kingdom of no sleep and thought" can be crossed only by spirits, but never by "living beings", in order to prevent the disruption of an unknown millennial energy stability.

A Sufi legend says that "The advent of Mahdi will happen. He did not disappear. He was simply ordered to go and live in the desert of Rub Al-Khali (The Empty Quarter). It is the desert of nothingness. Nobody can go there because of its quicksand and if you set foot there, you will be swallowed by the sands. There is a very big cave which hosts Qubbat-us-Sa'dat (the Dome of Happiness) which was built by angels. It is there that Mahdi and his 99 Caliphs live.

When Mahdi comes, Jesus will be with him, together with other people coming from different places around this Earth. There are so many unknown worlds around ours. Yet, Truth is one. This goes for everybody whether Muslims, Jewish or Christians."

Truth is One.

OR TRUTH!
WE PERCEIVE ONLY WHAT WE SEE
AND NOT WHAT IS THERE

Younis Tawfik an Iraqi writer, journalist and professor of Arabic language and literature at the University of Genoa, is an expert in the history and legends of the Rub Al-Khali (The Empty Quarter). He says:

"The Rub Al-Khali is a real legend in Arabic literature. It is known that Arabic poetry had its origins in the pre-Islamic period, in the form of long poems which were transmitted and preserved orally. Subsequently, with the arrival of writing, poetry became a kind of epic folklore among other stories. One of those poems tells the story of a man who tries to cross the Rub Al-Khali in an attempt to get the dowry for his bride. The crossing, however, becomes a superhuman adventure, which is practically impossible to achieve. All of his friends die and he remains alone and imprisoned in the quicksand. In the end, and only because of his bravery and heroism, his almost divine body is able to overcome this extremely difficult ordeal.

There are many other stories about people who have gone missing there. The Bedouins consider crossing the Empty Quarter as a challenge without any return and it is exactly for this reason that they only travel around it, never daring to take the risk of setting foot in it. It is said that in that desert there are very high dunes, colour-changing sand, strong winds, and quicksand. It is similar to the Bermuda Triangle, but has a more mysterious and dangerous aspect. There are innumerable legends about this desert which date back to the pre-Islamic era and are still known today. We can say that the latest attempt to cross this desert was made by a group of Saudi, Egyptian, American, Swiss, and German researchers who took cars, equipment and technologically advanced vehicles with them, which then broke down.

They covered three thousand kilometers in an attempt to be first ones to discover the treasures of this desert. Apart from the high dunes and quicksand, that desert has areas with waterfalls, a lake and residential places concentrated within the outer limits of Rub Al-Khali, but not inside it.

It is difficult to cross, if not impossible.

The desert is a large area equivalent to the surface of France, Belgium and the Netherlands put together. This is why there may be some areas that are rich in water and others where water is nowhere to be found. This makes that place impossible to explore. This research proves, however, that it is impossible for any human being to endure and survive the Rub Al-Khali without being equipped with vehicles and technologically advanced means. The heat, in some hours of the day, reaches very high temperatures with very strong winds that move the sands from one place to another on dunes as high as the Eiffel Tower. It is to be taken into consideration that the team of 32 experts who tried to cross the desert in 2005 were accompanied by guides, drivers, and doctors, so there was a team of 89 people to assist the experts. Despite all this, it proved impossible even for them to cross the largest desert in the world.

Taking all the above into consideration, I think that Max Calderan is an extraordinary person with superhuman powers, inspired by God. In order to cross this desert, a person must be a real human machine to endure thirst, hunger, sleep and to be able to walk

1,200 kilometres across dunes and areas which are unbearably hot during the day.

We will witness an impossible adventure which, in addition to being a challenge to science and nature, will prove that Max Calderan can do something that no other human has ever been able to achieve before.

So, I guess Max is the first and last person to accomplish such a feat and I think he is endowed with very high spiritual powers and needs the assistance of someone up there in the sky to help him finish such an adventure safe and sound."

Preparation for such an event is not easy. I have always believed that preparation should be phased building up gradually in difficulty and in the itinerary. This preparation is similar to the planning behind anything else in life, like a trip, a work day or shopping at the supermarket because in these cases, the person knows where to go, what to do and buy. Even if the technical difficulty is something you can organise and prepare for, the technical aspect becomes the least important part when you go against the legend of a place.

There is nothing technical about legends. Therefore, approaching the legend from a technical perspective, together with the addition of unexpected problems, will mean losing the battle right from the start. It is impossible to cut the air with a knife and this impossibility can be applied to the context of my explorations. Working with my team, we calculated that crossing the whole desert would take nearly forty days which brought to mind the 40 days in which Jesus was tempted by the devil in the desert. We had already been conditioned. Later on, after some brief incursions along the borders of the Rub Al-Khali and a series of stringent training, besides being an unconditioned explorer, I was convinced by practical savvy that I could have finished this challenge in less than 20 days. Recent tests prove that I could cross this desert faster than the scheduled time.

Actually, a legend about the Rub Al-Khali says that at some point I will reach the realm of the "asleeping" where it is impossible to sleep because, it is said, the watcher demon would take over the sleeping person's soul and would never let it go. According to this legend and from experience, the approach to this challenge will initially be very technical, just like in my other feats. I will start the challenge with a GPS, a backpack, food and water, until I get to the point where the team can no longer follow me and I will start my single-handed exploration of the Rub Al-Khali. I might meet some legendary figures and feel presences which are quite real, yet visible perhaps only in my mind and feelings. In order to face these presences, I must never allow myself to be conditioned and the only thing I have to think about is covering the itinerary, kilometer after kilometer without stopping until I reach a pre-established point where my team can follow me once again in their vehicles. This can come about only after I cover 400 km in complete solitude.

It is obvious that I will be more vulnerable due to physiological needs and emotional conditions such as hunger, thirst, pain, sleep, panic, vision, hearing, touch and taste. These situations can be managed only through absolutely perfect preparation and training that allows me to do without drinking or eating while covering up to 100 kilometers in less than 24 hours. This will serve me when dealing with extreme situations in which I have to consume very little water and food, if any at all is left, for up to seven days at a time.

I have changed a lot of my workouts and applied several

modifications to them, after the 2012 attempt which had to be stopped 270 kilometres into the challenge due to a sandstorm. My fixed goal is to develop the ability to manage a complete lack of water and food, complete sleep deprivation and prolonged, extreme efforts. The Rub Al-Khali is defined as the point of no return. Now, I am aware that in fact the point of no return was related to the plight of people who, in the past, did not have the same medical and scientific opportunities as we do today, neither did they have as good a knowledge of the territory that we now have thanks to the use of satellites.

The only thing I wonder about is how many days it will take me to complete the challenge, but not whether I will be able to make it or not.

THE SCIENTIFIC POINT OF VIEW
SCIENCE CAN EXPLAIN EVERYTHING
UNTIL WE HAVE TO ASK FOR GOD'S HELP

The most surprising thing in these extreme challenges in places where no other human has ever been able to set foot, is that we can reach a limit that stands between science and something else. There are no scientific studies about athletic exasperation in extreme environments, except those carried out in controlled environments where the athlete's health is the only priority. Being controlled, these conditions lack the distinguishing variable of the instinct to survive.

I manage sleep by applying a dietary principle which is unique in the world, combining the micro-cycle sleep method with carbohydrate-free snacks to avoid alteration in blood sugar levels and the subsequent release of insulin, which is the hormone that destabilises energy performance.

In today's society, we are increasingly subjected to stressful situations. Assessment of how stress affects the nervous system of an athlete facing extreme conditions, could be useful to understand if personal genetics can manage this impact with stress hormones, such as cortisol, which is known for reducing lifespan. It would be great to make a synthesis of what are presented to us as separate parts: body and mind.

Zealous supporters of traditional medicine and those of homeopathy are two never-meeting currents. A person needs enormous physical effort and great faith in the desert. Revealing medical data about myself has been given to me. However, these data are of no importance to me, no matter how significant they are. I have been found to have a perfect heart which is exactly the same as that of an eighteen-year old boy and in the same condition as an unused organ.

It has been discovered that my sleep during my feats is similar to that of dolphins, in which half a hemisphere is asleep while the other half is awake, which then switch roles. This condition allows me to walk non-stop while being apparently asleep. It has been found that my lung capacity is normal except for the fact that I use 100% of it. I have undergone a complete DNA mapping which gave standard results. All my internal organs are in normal condition.

The difference is in the synchronous and harmonious use of my organs in order to achieve excellent performance. It is the same as playing the seven music notes one at a time, which is an easy thing to do, while creating harmonious music is a more difficult task. We have to be dedicated, have inspiration or be inspired. There are so many tips which are given, irresponsibly so, simply because theoretical suggestions have never been practically applied in the midst of the desert.

I found it hard to question studies about amino-acids, vitamins, hormones, the importance of carbohydrates and training tables when I discovered that all you need to gain the independence necessary to run tens of hours to cover 400 kilometers on dunes and at a temperature that can reach 58 degrees, is to eat few dates, drink camel milk and wear a pair of shoes that are worth only 15 euro.

Along my way, I have understood that necessity is primarily based on the most updated scientific knowledge, which is very useful and irreplaceable by invalidated theories. This instrument can be used to make a leap ahead, that is, to use science and what we know about physical knowledge in order to create one's own method and lifestyle, so we can stand out. We have to be aware that there is no universal method. There are however, as many methods as there are bodies and souls on this planet.

I normally eat a bit of everything, but limit my consumption of carbohydrates because I am not a fan of pasta. I eat small quantities of whatever I crave. When I finish eating, I must not be overfull and I must be able to start running as fast as I would if I were being chased by a wild animal. I only eat as much food as to allow me to able to do everything I want. I eat when I am hungry and I drink when I feel thirsty. It is far easier than you may imagine. It is the easiest thing in the world to eat when you are hungry and drink when you feel thirsty (whether you are suffering from a disease or not).

IMPOSSIBLE TO FORGET
FOCUS ON YOUR PROJECTS RATHER THAN ON YOUR MEMORIES

In his book "The Seven Pillars of Wisdom", Lawrence says "Bedouin ways were hard even for those brought up with them and for foreigners they were terrible: a death in life".

It is true that nobody could lead this life in a desert and remain unchanged. Even when you feebly feel it, the image of the desert Bedouins will remain with you, together with the desire to return to that place, because these stones and sands can take cruel hold over you in an incomparable way. The life of the Bedouins in the desert have such a strong impression on a person that it changes them completely.

Once I felt a benevolent envy towards the Bedouins. It was in Oman, and I saw a Bedouin standing, motionless, on top of a huge dune. The sun had just set and the twilight tinged the sands with a reddish colour. It seemed as if it were moving as the hues of the sunset changed.

It was time for the afternoon prayer (As-Salat) which can be prayed from sunset until the red twilight disappears from the horizon. It seemed like only on that dune could the Bedouin receive a beam of light directly from heaven, fully enveloping and protecting him. While he was praying, he recited some verses from the Quran and his voice sounded so heavenly that it seemed as if it were coming directly from the Universe. His was not just a voice, but a divine sound mingled with an earthly swish that created a melody which needed no other accompaniment than the wind, which gently moved the Bedouin's words into the mysterious desert. The energy surrounding the Bedouin was so strong that might I have tried to hit him with a stick, it would have bounced back and been pulverised. Helpless and impressed at the same time, I stood there watching him from afar. I envied him for his indissoluble power which I realised that I possessed, though only up to a certain extent. Yes, I was strong, but even if that Bedouin might not have been able to cross the desert alone, he had something more than me. That something was the full protection of God and his prayer was the means to receive it.

I studied very assiduously to become better acquainted with religions. I came to the conclusion that each and every location has its history and culture and, with them, its own religion which triggers deep emotions that emerge through prayers like the Gregorian Chant, the Buddhist Nam-Myoho-Renge Kyo chant, the Latin Pater Noster prayer, the Quran verses and the Jewish tefillah prayer in the Siddur, to name a few.

The sounds evoked by reciting millennial prayers can have the same strong emotional influence as that of a song which can make us cry when we listen to it on the radio. When I pray alone or with the Bedouins in the desert, I always feel an immense emotion and a protective power engulfs me and accompanies me in the dunes.

In Oman, amongst the sands of the Tropic of Cancer, I met a nomad who lived with his family in a tent. They moved *house* to wherever they could take their goats and camels. His name was Ahmed and he was taken aback when he heard me speaking his language and even more when he heard what name the Bedouins had given me: Mahdi Abdullah.

His face was deeply wrinkled and sunburned, and he walked on the stones barefoot. Amazed at seeing me walking alone, he offered me hospitality and shelter in his tent to protect me from the sun. Inside, his wives and their three children sat in respectful silence. His wives were covered with a veil which barely showed their eyes. We talked very little. There among the dunes where solitude is the only thing you can come across for months and months, silence becomes the noblest form of respect reserved for a guest to avoid embarrassment. Ahmed lit a fire, and touched every single object slowly with precise movement as if he were touching relics.

Even the tea, which was poured from high above the cup to enhance its flavour, seemed as if it had been controlled by a mysterious force that prevented it from spilling out of the cup. Everything in that tent was clean, even if the cups and pot had not been washed in a dishwasher. Everything was in good harmony. The only sound in that paradise was the sound of the soft wind which occasionally brought gusts of warmth onto our faces. The floor was made of carpets that had been worn out by time rather than by being trodden on. On one of those carpets there was a huge plate full of couscous and gazelle meat cut into medium-size chunks. Outside the tent, there were strips of meat covered with salt and spices and left hanging to dry. There was a hole in the ground where I could see glowing embers made with dry bushes and palm trunks, and from which, Ahmed drew some bread that had been freshly-baked in a sand oven. We all kneeled in a circle around that dish and I really felt at home.

Only after having recited some verses of the Quran to thank Allah (God) for the food and health he bestowed on us, did we start to eat. No cutlery is used in the desert and people eat using their right hand as far as possible because the left hand is considered the hand of the devil (Shaitan). A small portion of couscous and meat is placed in the hand, forming the shape of a small ball which is held with the fingertips and put in the mouth while whispering "Bismillah" (in the name of God).

That food seemed as if it were life and not simply food. Nobody there ate greedily, no matter how hungry they were. The body is nourished without anxiety or haste. It is inevitable that those people react differently to hunger and thirst, due to their habit of prolonged fasting and the difficulty in obtaining food and water. Sleep also is faced differently, since there is no electricity and the day-night cycle depends on sunrise and sunset. Ahmed had a proud and confident look which shone on his face full of wrinkles conceived by the difficult and harsh life of a nomad. Ahmed could still not understand how I was able to go alone into the desert without even the company of a camel.

The desert is ruthless and this was why Ahmed warmly urged me to divert my walk towards another track where I could find recent traces to follow. In reply, always speaking in Arabic, I told him that I had had a camel, but since she was a female and talked too much, I had buried her in the sand and set off alone. After a moment's hesitation, we all burst out laughing. Ahmed's wife laughed lowering her face, but keeping her eyes up so I was able to see, through the opening in her veil, their expression of joy and entertainment. The children giggled and put their hands on their mouths to cover their smiles and their very white teeth. Ahmed gave me a big hug and said peremptorily "Al Hamdulillah" (Thanks be to God). I turned around and went on my way, turning now and then to look at that tent which gradually started to fade behind the twisted columns of the heat of the scorching stones. That scene, unchanged and unchanging, has been repeated in the desert for thousands of years. I had read so much about it in books, but living those moments first-hand gives such a greater excitement that you do not want to go back home because you realise that being happy is not based on anything material. In those moments, silence is the best word and nudity is real clothing.

Again, I was alone, no tent, no family and no camel. My pace became heavier on the stones which gave way to the sand, metre after metre. It was so hot that I had to stop. I chose to stand because the ground was too hot to sit on. I closed my eyes and listened. When imaging the desert, we always think about the profound silence of the desert that is almost deafening and about the disorientation by the absence of any background noise whatsoever! No sound to indicate the presence of a human being or of the blood flowing your veins.

Very few people know that heat has its own sound which can be perceived only in the vibrations it makes. It is so strong that it engulfs you and penetrates into every pore in your body and the feeling is just like when you emerge your body into a boiling tub of water. When you breathe it in, you can feel it moving into your body until it reaches the last bronchiole of your lungs, suffocating you with a burning sensation if you try to inhale through your mouth.

Unlike the wind, the desert summer heat does not have any sound, but when it overwhelms you, you instinctively tremble like a mad person to shake it off your body. You would plug your ears with your fingers and hands to stifle it and scream louder than the heat, imploring it to end, although it is somewhat contradictory to close your ears to stop feeling the heat.

Then night falls and it is cold, like the chills that run through your skin. I have lit so many fires in the dark desert nights. What I remember most is when I lit a fire with a shy fennec fox nearby. The animal stayed close by until it was startled by a strong flame from the fire.

Fire evokes mixed feelings: the feeling of vitality, safety, control and power in the part of your body facing the flames, while the feeling behind you is that of a relentless cold, the freezing air coming from the darkest of the dark which is so frightening that it makes you afraid even of turning around to see what it is like. Anything can approach you in the pitch-dark night, but you would not realise it until it jumped on you. Therefore, we should turn our backs to the fire to keep our back warm whilst keeping a look out for any danger that may arrive from nowhere to catch you unaware in the dark.

In our daily life, we tend to do just the opposite, that is we turn our backs to the various dangers around us and take refuge in the apparent safety of something we can recognise.

I have never been afraid. Darkness enhances all dormant senses. However, one night something unexpected happened which radically changed my already scrupulous preparation. The batteries of the GPS (similar to the navigation systems used in cars) died and I had to stop and sit down on the rocks to replace them. My hands were shaking so hard because of the fever I had. My fever was caused by strong heat during the day, which then turned into strong teeth-chattering and shivering. I removed the four dead batteries, put them on the ground and took four new ones from my backpack. I was trembling so hard that the new batteries fell on the ground, got mixed up with the old ones and I had no other charged batteries. What a tragedy! This meant I had to make infinite attempts to see which were the charged batteries that would make the GPS work again. I made the first attempt but my hands were shaking so hard that the batteries and the GPS kept falling on the ground. At the same time, the lamp I had on my forehead switched off. Another dead battery and another tragedy. I was alone and had a fever of 40 degrees. The temperature outside was 5 degrees, and I had no GPS, no light and no water. The chilly wind stopped me from thinking. I had convulsions because of the cold weather and I heard the steps of an animal. I felt a cold hand caressing my face, heard voices whispering in my ear and I saw lights and colours mixed with the sand which moved with the wind and started to cover me.

That night, I realised that the first thing to do when stopping in the desert at night is to light a small fire. I also learned that dead batteries must immediately be put aside before taking out the new ones. A small unexpected situation could lead to a tragedy. When all alone, I often think about the fact that everything could end in a moment, that my heart could rip because of the fatigue I feel, just like I do when I climb dunes as high as twenty-storey buildings in the middle of summer. I keep my head down and walk step by step. My foot sinks in the sand, pulling me down and obliging me to stay in the same spot. My leg also sinks up to the knee. I find it more difficult to pull my leg out of the sand than to take the next step, which in its turn, sinks deep down in the sand. I stick my hands into it to help me in my walk, but they also get burned in the hot sands. I stare upwards and all I can see is an endless wall and then the sky above everything. I climb step by step with my heart beating even faster. I begin breathing faster and to the extent that I start to breathe through my mouth, so boiling air mixed with fine dust are inhaled, reaching my lungs and burning them. I sometimes feel so exhausted that I collapse on the sand and feel even weaker when my body comes into contact with that source of 50 degree heat. Once I reach the top, I discover that there is nothing but other dunes ahead of me.

At night when I am overcome with sleep, I lie down and look at the sky and feel as if the stars are within reach. The stars look even brighter in the pitch darkness. They are everywhere in the sky and I see them all along the horizon. The sky above is so limpid that it seems as if I can see galaxies and nebula with the naked eye. All of a sudden, I see the glowing tail of a falling star which disappears just as I make a wish or a satellite which is visible to the naked eye, though somewhat less romantic.

I lie down on the sand and wonder how I am refreshed by this same sand that burns me during the day. I hold the sand in my hands and let it slip in through my fingers. I wonder how many people have observed this same sky that I am looking at now. I think about all the things that inspired man and made him study the stars which formed various constellations, the phases of the moon as well as the stars the Bedouins and caravans used as the only compass and tool to find their way to oases where they could find water and survive in the desert. I tried plotting the stars on a sheet of paper and pretending I was an ancient Egyptian, but all my efforts went in vain. The task was too complicated and there were too many stars in the sky. It is impossible to pinpoint the zodiac signs or understand that the North Star is immobile, and that the moon has different phases. If I want to understand something, I have to do this spontaneously without forcing myself to do so. Something much greater than me can show me the way. The only thing I have to do is to be sincere in asking.

I felt as if the answers to my questions were up there in that sky, but I could not see them with the naked eye. I believed I was free despite having the feeling of being watched over. I realised that life here is straightforward and there was no barrier between me and the Universe or between me and God. I felt so tiny and came to realise that this earthly journey cannot end with our physical existence. I felt so happy and content being wrapped up in this solitude. I had the feeling of being immortal. I was immediately overwhelmed with the desire to go back home and tell my loved once about my feelings, while sitting there around a fireplace with all my family close by. Our thoughts travel, they are created and then destroyed. Thousands of images come to me of my past, present and future life, of pain, joy, memories even of the time when I was in my mother's womb, my dreams, my life and feelings.

The cold wind dies down and the night is covered with silence and quiet. Everything stands still. Everything. Reality appears differently, it looks dramatic and bound to end forever.

I felt dehydrated and exhausted, so I laid down completely naked on the ground in an attempt to cool down. The more I cooled down the better I felt. I felt free to swim in the universe amongst the stars that I continued to observe. I deliberately chose that place on top of the dune so I could free myself even if, deep down in my heart, I always felt there was another hardship waiting for me. I expected someone from above to fetch me and let me end this short earthly trip. My body was empty and motionless. The only thing that broke the silence was my slow heart beat (it signalled 12 beats per minute). Then, my heart beat came to a stop as well. I started to flow amongst the stars and galaxies and was accompanied by a voice that advised me to be patient while running towards the Truth.

I reached the farthest planets of the Universe and found myself in other civilisations, other worlds and ended up in "my" Rub Al-Khali where I saw myself along among thousands of unexplored dunes, unshaven, skinny, with no food nor waterand free even from the slavery of sleep. I walked without leaving any footprints. I was enveloped in a bright light which dazzled and protected me at the same time.

"This *is* the Way, the only way. Now, go back". These are the only words I distinctly remember hearing during that trip.

A cartographer of a famous oil company studied all the sharp and precise details I described to him. He repeatedly asked me "How could you remember all these particular details about the Rub Al-Khali?" I still wonder how.

It seemed as if I had a spotlight fixed onto my eyes. My awakening coincided with the rise of the moon which wasn't full. Then the whistle of the wind and even my thirst became tangible once again.

I got dressed again and made a huge effort to reach the top of the dune. From afar, I saw a spot of moving light. It was a trail connecting two oases. It looked as if a SUV might have passed on that trail. I used the stars as my guide to set my direction and the next morning I reached the water well that saved my life.

In the desert, night has always been magical and mysterious. Anything could happen at night, even an encounter with the "Children of the Night" as they are still called. They are kind of ghost Bedouins who used to attack caravans, disappearing suddenly in the night, without leaving any trace. Caravans full of spices and precious stones, travelling for more than 70 days from Cairo (Egypt) were very attractive to those robbers who considered themselves to be the owners of everything that crossed their deserts.

A journey along the Great Caravan Route in the Arabian Peninsula needed more than 2,500 camels and was the source of a revenue equivalent to 60 million euro. I would not be surprised if, one day, I stumble on a stone and find out that it is the tip of a pyramid. The dunes change shape and colour in just few hours. Just imagine how many things these dunes have covered over the centuries, things that will never be found. Researches and explorers, especially in the last century, let themselves be guided by very simple stories, mostly Arabian, which had been handed down through generations. One of the stories speaks about an alleged existence of a huge treasure hidden in the sands. In the Book of Buried Pearls (tales from old Persia), a father tells his son "Along the way, you will see date palms, vines and water springs, then you will find an narrow road which will take you to the city, but you will find the city gates locked. On the gate you will see a stone sculpture of a bird. Put your hand into its open beak and take the key kept there. Open the gate and enter the city. There you will find incredible treasures." The city has never been found because we often forget that the desert carefully hides whatever it wants to conceal.

Things may look similar to a layman's eyes, but the dunes take different shapes and are classified by type: there are the barchans which are horse-shoe shaped; the Zamba dunes which have a rocky formation; the Edeyen dunes which are flat and consistent; the Ighidi dunes made of fine and soft grains of sand and difficult to cross with a four-wheeler; the Stellar dunes which are formed by the wind blowing in different directions, giving the dune the shape of a huge star as well as the Chain dunes made of long lines of compact and accessible corridors of sand and gravel. It is very difficult to move from one dune to another. Besides, deposits of very fine sands, similar to talc powder, accumulate at the base of the dunes. These deposits can easily bury a two meter long iron shovel. I am 1,80 m tall and should therefore avoid quicksand because I could literally be swallowed and disappear without a trace.

Eventually, though, everything is counterbalanced in the land of the Arabian Nights, the ancient homeland of incense and myrrh. Oman, Yemen, Saudi Arabia, Qatar, Bahrain, and the Emirates are a real discovery in a magical atmosphere full of emotions that we come across only in films. This is the land where fantasy sailors landed, the land where barefoot sultans riding unicorns used to run in the wilderness, the land where the Queen of Sheba met King Solomon. It is the land of history and legends, reality and make-believe, which have all fascinated the most unconventional travellers. This is the land that can thrills us even with a simple organised excursion. This place is part of my journey, but it would not make me forget my origin and roots. However, all things considered, I sometimes long for a refreshing thunderstorm after having suffered the strong heat in my challenges.

SPONSORS
YOU CAN LIVE WITHOUT SIBLINGS
BUT NOT WITHOUT FRIENDS (ARABIC PROVERB)

A general reflection about the sponsors who try to make business out of a feat or sporting event, and about why a person needs an investor to make their dream come true. Nothing is impossible once you have made up your mind to take it on. The most fundamental thing is that we ourselves are our own real sponsors.

These reflections are addressed to all of those who invest their lives in reaching their ideals or accomplishing projects which could enable them to improve themselves or the lives of others, but do not have the financial resources to achieve what they want.

Logically speaking, in very simple terms, a company sponsors an event or an athlete because it wants an advantage in visibility, to increase revenue and improve its image. A company or an individual may invest money for the sole aim of making a financial profit without necessarily needing to appear publicly.

It happens that when asking for sponsorship or investment, our request is refused in 99% of the cases. The answer might be "Sorry, we do not have enough money in our budget; We are not interested; Let us think it over next year; We can provide technical assistance but not financing and so on".

Then, you might find that the same potential sponsor/investor you contacted, has financed an event which is similar, if not equal, to yours. You may even learn that that sponsor/investor has spent five times the amount you had asked for.

Why does this happen?

Emotionally speaking, the person who lives this experience cannot find any plausible or valid justification. Some might say that things would have been different and an investor could have easily be found if we lived in the USA or in a country of Sheikhs. So, the refusal is caused by the fact we are living in Italy, for example, and not because of the proposal itself. This can clearly explain why so many "brains" flee Italy in search of resources and, most importantly, to find a place where they can create their dreams. However, this does not explain why another person was able to get sponsorship, while we could not. Allow me tell you what the word sponsor/investor means to me. "Sponsors and investors" are all those who believe in what we do, who do not hinder our endeavours, who show real interest in what we do and give us a hand in making our dream come true (like starting a shop, getting a degree, learning a language or even achieving a simple desire) by, let's say, giving us a ride to railway station because our car has broken down.

The first true supporters of our dreams are those who are close to us. The most important thing for us is to truly believe in what we do and have and unshakable faith that our dream can come true. The issue regarding how to make this happen is the fruit of a precise and well-planned programme to follow.

Much mental and logical organisation, rather than feelings, is needed to rationally manage an emotional and enthusiastic drive. It is extremely important to set a clear goal, plan a budget in terms of calculating all the resources needed to achieve our goal, which are not only economical. This can be applied to all goals be it to lose 20 kilos of weight or open a business, for example. Let us be surrounded by our true and first sponsors and investors, that is, those who truly believe in what we do, and let us keep those who frustrate our plans well away. Let us choose which direction we have to take to make our dreams come true and which doors will most likely open when we knock on them. Let us avoid wasting time on newspaper chronicles that only consume our energy and creativity.

Let us stop and think for ourselves and carefully listen to the news bulletins, noting down how long we dedicate to each bulletin as well as the issues covered: politics, chronicles, gossip, fashion, sports, economy, scandals. Only after we have read everything over, can we make a frank decision about which news and advertising information are really useful to improve the quality of our life, find solutions to a problem or give a full reply to a question we have. Let us decide for ourselves which news and advertising information is worth knowing, deserving of deeper understanding and what we think is definitely useful. This simple exercise made me realise how many watts are consumed by listening to the news which I then use in my everyday conversations, consuming thus more energy which I could use differently, that is in achieving my goals.

Probably those who achieve a goal have pursued a different path from ours, presented it differently and have sacrificed a lot of time without wasting any of it sitting in front of the television or perhaps they have never let things go. Those people must have always been defiant, determined, full of unwavering faith and passion, and must have dedicated their time to finding solutions rather than speaking about obstacles, problems or bad news.

We are all much greater than we think! Let us rebel silently. Let us break the chains that make us dominated by other people's thoughts. Let us use those thoughts in other reflections, if necessary. There's no need for street rallies, nor for meetings with yelling politicians as there's no need to change someone's opinion simply because they are different from us, apparently.

Instead, let us rebel against the people we see when we look at the mirror and find someone else. Sometimes the first one to be unsupportive is ourself. The mirror reflects just a container that holds a huge amount of untapped potential. We must begin by looking for it and starting to consciously filter everything we perceive.

Choosing to make a change does not begin in a polling station, but inside of us when we cast our first vote of preference.

Let us give our vote to our soul which already has a perfect, indestructible and eternal plan, called self-love, instinct for survival, passion, faith and life.

This will be the first real contract you have with a sponsor.

THE SOLUTION
"SHOW US THE STRAIGHT PATH" (the Quran I,6)

The answer is always in the question. When we are afraid of huge obstacles in our way, we always forget how weak they are and how we can destroy them in an instant. We should learn from idioms and proverbs because they always have an element of truth: "the giant with feet of clay", "Achilles' heel" as well as "the mouse that scares the elephant" are just few examples to take into consideration. Even the worst of enemies has a weak point. The biggest problems can be destroyed in a heartbeat, once their weakness has been discovered. How can we solve global problems of war, killings, denial of rights, debts, racism and such? I think that the way to do this for believers like Christians, Hebrews, Muslims, Hindus or Buddhists, to name a few, is to strictly observe the precepts and/or commandments they received. As for the non-believers, I would suggest that they apply the rule, which is always valid, that states that our freedom to act ends where that of others begins. This rule is valid for all of us. Without distinction, "eleventh commandment" could be applied to invite people to do their own business in order to find a solution to everything though this could be a very complicated issue as history has proved it. However, we all have to give it a try.

In Jerusalem, during the "Run for Love" press conference, I called on the greatest politicians on Earth to sit together at a table and simply talk about their families, children, hobbies and such, rather than discuss how to solve conflicts in the world or the issue of the Middle East, and I am sure they would have found things in common between them. Then I invited the most powerful people on Earth– not in the Universe- to reflect on something. I said "Imagine if, during your meeting in this highly-technological room, a small number of women and children who have been mutilated or disfigured by bombs had been invited to sit next to your wives and mothers. Now, give the order to launch a missile at a the house next door to yours, where a dreadful terrorist lives! You should not have any doubt or fear regarding the outcome of this operation, since these missiles are known as "intelligent bombs" and are perfectly capable of hitting their targets, leaving innocent people unharmed. Not surprisingly, because your loved ones are involved, an alternative solution would be found almost magically not only to save them, but so as to benefit everyone. Since it is believed that the beating of a butterfly's wings in Australia can trigger a hurricane in the USA, I would suggest letting a gnat beats its wings in your small vegetable patch. Allow me to suggest a very simple way that can demolish the global system of deception that I tried to describe in this book in few seconds. It could be through the resizing of personal ambitions and the practice of favouritism of those few people who would not mind ending the lives of innocent citizens who have always maintained a system with their sacrifices. We could see fear grow on the faces of the arrogant "powerful" people who would panic at the idea of losing control and, consequently, the power to manipulate other people. It is time to surprise them like dumping a bucket of cold water and a bolt from the blue."

It is time to react and make a quick change of direction towards the Light. It might seem strange not to have thought about this simple method before. The funny thing is that the means to break down the whole global system is provided by the same people who command the World and impose their entrapping rules on it. It is a method that does not foresee revolutions, rallies, rebellions, breaking the law, blatant shouting and gestures, acts of violence, verbal attacks, public expression of opinion, acts of hatred nor robbing anybody. It is a system that nobody on this Earth can destroy, not even by the so-called "Powerful Ones".

This method is called *"respecting the rules"*. Yes, *respecting the rules*. The rules imposed by "society" can resolve its own complete collapse. The answer is *always* in the question. Love is the surge that can make this method succeed. We have to love and care for ourselves. Dear *"Powerful of the Earth"*, since you care so much about us and about our future, we will literally respect the tips and rules you give us to show you our gratitude. We will be very accurate and scrupulous in observing all the laws and rules of conduct you implement to improve our life and that of our children. We wholeheartedly thank you for having shown us the way. I know that this may sound impossible, but respecting the rules will make the whole system collapse of its own accord. Can you imagine using *love* to open a rift in the biggest dam ever built by man? This rift will be the beginning to the thunderous destruction of the cage which we are all locked up in. Am I a fool? A wishful thinker? No, I am not. I am very down to earth, just like the steps I set when I walk in the desert. To prove what I am saying, let us think together and bring up a real example which is applicable to our daily lives as of tomorrow. Let me give a very simple example to illustrate how things work. Imagine that tomorrow, we all, yes *all*, will respect the highway code in Rome or Milan. This being the case, there will be no parking tickets, no speed limit violations detected by speed cameras and no breach of law to be fined for. The City Hall will run out of funds because of this full compliance with the rules. A full compliance with the traffic code for one month will make it impossible for the City Hall to pay the salaries of its own employees, including the sky-high salaries of managers and consultants.

Let us add all the other related expenses: the tow car and the money to be paid for it, lawyers' fees and calls for appeal and expenses run up in cafés and restaurants near the appeal courts. If full compliance with the speed limit will reduce or even eliminate traffic accidents, then we must also take another thing into account. Let us think about the number of people who go are taken to the emergency room after minor traffic accidents, creating thus more revenue for the pharmaceutical companies that deal with medicine and medication. Think about how much money is spent at health stores on braces, crutches, wheelchairs and other such aids; at rehabilitation centres to cure limbs; for claiming accident compensation from insurance companies; at showrooms to replace the damaged car with a new one or at car repair shops to fix cars that were damaged because they were parked badly. Think about the days you are unable to work, too. The whole economy of a company, the so-called Municipality of Rome or Milan, would collapse if we fully observed the rules which protect our health and which we should abide by, simply because we love ourselves and do not want to put our lives, safety and salaries at risk. If we all fully complied with the highway code in Italy, there would be an impossible-to-solve national crisis. The system would spontaneously implode if we observed the highway code. This is a real, solid example. A lot of money is involved. Don't you believe me? The Municipality of

Rome pockets 231,706,163 euro a year from fines. Besides this fact, the revenues of other small municipalities located by a busy motorway have increased their income from local taxes seven-fold (source: Il Sole 24 Ore).

The village of San Giovanni Lipione in the province of Chieti has 287 inhabitants who pay taxes amounting to 49,683 euro per year. Annual revenues from fines reached 355,000 euro in 2006, which equates to 714% of their budget. Villanova Biellese in the province of Biella, which has only 177 inhabitants, collects 68,599 euro of taxes a year and its annual revenue from fines is 356,814 euro, which is 520% of its total income. Italian law dictates that revenue from fines is to be used in observance of article 208, which of course, is never complied with. 80% of the revenues owed to the government should be spent on the National Plan for Road Safety, initiatives to promote road safety, road safety education and improvement of road signs.

However, the government can choose other ways to spend the money since there are no sanctions that oblige it not to do so. It can choose to spend the money differently, through the Ministry of Transport, being the authority in charge. The proceeds from fines collected by local authorities, should however be spent on improving and upgrading road signs, urban traffic plan, suburban roads, and road safety, with particular attention to be paid to vulnerable people like pedestrians, the elderly, cyclists and children. A law passed in 2005 states that at least 50% of revenue is to be spent on road safety courses at schools. Since there are no sanctions imposed on those who break the law, the local authorities choose to spend the money any way they want, perhaps on financing a "wine festival", for example. In all cases, we are the ones who are made to pay for this. Now you might be more convinced that the whole system could fall if we simply comply with the rules of the highway code which has been enacted to protect our health and fill their pockets. Paradoxically speaking, a meteorite crashing into earth would cause less damage than respecting the rules imposed by the Health and Public Health office. Yes! You are absolutely right. I will stop smoking to avoid having lung cancer. OK! I will stop overeating to avoid having diabetes, obesity, heart problems, blood pressure and cholesterol. Perfect! To play it safe, I will also watch less TV and exercise more.

 Hospitals will be overcrowded with patients who do not respect the rules. An international pharmaceutical system suggests some rules and certain lifestyle choices to prevent diseases, but if a patient does not respect the rules, why should he be mentally stressed by another international system until he collapses? This is where medicine is needed as a remedy. I will not mention any figures or numbers because they are far above our imagination. Yet, let us think about something 'Do you think that a multinational producer of medicines wants people to take precautions and care about their health?' or 'Do you think it is easier to give a solution that citizens can voluntarily adopt under false justification?' Who has not tried to escape from some pressing situations by taking refuge into the pleasures of eating? Who of us hasn't driven fast because they were late? How many of us gorge themselves with food knowing they can rely on a tablet to solve their indigestion? This is absolutely not the usual attack on multinationals. A lot of people fight multinationals, not knowing that the more they are attacked, the stronger they become, simply because the attackers will consume all their energy that would be better used to love themselves a bit more.

Pharmaceutical companies produce whatever they want, but in the end, we are the ones who buy their products. Half of the world is the seller and the other half is the buyer. Medicine is sold and bought with money and this is what is positive about this whole thing. Love, however, can be obtained free of charge. It cannot be bought but can be equally exchanged.

If we once again think about solving things with this commonplace method called "respecting the rules", we might consider implementing it in the Western world. Why not starting from Italy, for example, where this method could be officially implemented as a sort of "Ramadan" whith a month of full obedience of the rules.

Let us put an end to rallies, demonstrations, verbal attacks, prejudices and political parties. In this way, we will be able to prevent violent "Black-Block" attacks; traffic jams, anger for having to change itinerary and late arrival at work (speeding up) and overeating sweets and pastries as stress-related behaviour (as well as other medicines for headaches and high blood pressure or antibiotics, because the body immune defence is low and you have the flu, and so on). In this way, you are following the rules, so no one can ever stop you. No law can oblige you not to respect the rules! You are unassailable. In this way, the *giant with the feet of clay* will miserably collapse on the ground. I will continuously repeat this: *Love yourselves and respect yourselves. Take care of your bodies and souls. Do this with love. Show more respect to yourselves. Open your eyes to the obvious contradictions we see in our daily lives and which are there to make us explode.*

Love changes everything. Silence is the true and most noble form of rebellion. The worst situation a speaker can face is having an audience who is silent from the beginning to end and who leave without even uttering a word. This situation is much worse than having an audience of protestors who are then easily manipulated because someone broke a shop-window. A speaker without an audience is not an orator. Try to bear this in mind. Reality shows are broadcasted on TV because they have an audience and they will cease to exist if you change channel and stop watching them. You have to tailor your life according to your way of thinking, so If you think about a TV show, you will look for it and start to watch it. There will be nothing in your mind except for what is broadcasted on TV, yet you should be the ones who create what is broadcasted. Printed media is still too weak compared to television, which is the instrument used to manipulate those people who think they have freedom of choice. There is nothing else apart from what is broadcasted on television. The news we watch on TV is reflected in our daily life which, as mentioned above, is overwhelmed with stress, acceleration, alcohol, accidents, overeating, medicine, and debts. We eventually end up breaking the rules. I am not a rebel, protestor nor a biased politician. I am simply a man with a challenging path to walk in my life: a path full of affection, work and faith.

 Mistakes - *or opportunities*, depending on the beholder– have helped me to grow with a broad mind, which I have used for the improvement of this world. This is why I would never accept comments like *"What would you know about life if you have always been so lucky?"* I could have fallen into snares of despair or even could have taken my life, but I have decided to fight. The more difficulties I faced, the more I remembered the saying that *"The more the cod is beaten, the more delicious it becomes."* The more humiliations I faced, the better perception I had of things. The bigger the obstacles in my way, the more I realised that God was testing me. Now, I am thankful to all my life experiences, without which I would not have suffered and made others suffer, and I would not have been able to survive in deserts to carry a message of love to all the World. Jesus said "*It is not what goes into one's mouth that makes them unclean, but what comes out of it.*" However, there were no carcinogenic preservatives at the time of Jesus. Nowadays, we have to try to stay clean and carefully select the food we eat. What comes out of our mouth is the outcome of our thoughts, regardless of whether we are free or conditioned. I have developed a personal perception of the subtle mechanism of the "*world-system theory*" and of its followers. Ever since I was a child, I understood that a believer is taught to pray to God to ask Him for help. A person would be easily considered as mad if he claimed to have seen Jesus, enveloped in a bright light and to have spoken to Him. So, just imagine, after all the sun and the heat I have been exposed to, what heresies would be blamed on me, I, the "*king of the desert*". It would be said that I have spoken to the greatest prophets who came to Earth, from Moses to Jesus to Mohammed. As it would be said that I knew the prophets were coming back and that some of them were already here. It would also be said that I know that the Messiah's return is not a legend and that he is hiding in the sands of the Empty Quarter, waiting for a signal to leave his hiding place and emerge. Too much is said but too little is done. Let us be the first to keep our mouths shut and start to love. Little lights can be seen much more clearly in the pitch dark. Light will guide us in life and love will give us strength.

LOVE
FELT AND THOUGHT ABOUT

A lot of choices, whether right or wrong, have been made in the name of love, which is then revealed to be unreal.

There is a big difference between "feeling" like acting on it somehow and "thinking" that there is a better way to do things, and vice versa.

It often happens that we say "I felt" I should not have done it, but I acted upon what I "thought" was the right thing to do. Or else, we may say "I think" it is not right for me to go this way, but "I feel" like an inner voice is telling me to move in that direction. Our thoughts are then mingled with those of the others. Thus, we may say "I felt" it was right to do something, but I did not do it because "everybody thought" it was wrong and told me to let it go.

We are all slaves to classical friendly guidance, such as *"Forget about that woman or man. She or he is not the right person for you. You're so different!"* You might listen to this, even if deep down, you "feel" despite the apparent diversity, there is an irrational common vibration between you.

There is big difference between "thinking" about doing something and "feeling" like doing it, since the former involves the left hemisphere of the brain, the rational part, while the latter involves the right hemisphere of the brain that deals with emotions.

Thanks to the help of a researcher and a genetics laboratory, I was able to improve my scientific knowledge about the relations that may exist between DNA, the frequencies it generates, and what we consider *love*.

My goal was to rationally understand the mechanism that leads us to be attracted to some people rather than others (a kind of stroll, in fact). It is one of those ideas that spring to mind while shopping at the supermarket or jogging in the park!. I came to the conclusion that our decision to get to know someone better is triggered by specific choices we make in the very first moment of a new encounter.

When two people meet, they look at each other for first time and their subconscious reaction in the right hemisphere of their brains creates frequencies, images or unconditioned feelings in the first tenth of a second of their encounter. It is at that very moment that we feel the correlation between the essence of that person and ours, and understand their true nature in the deepest possible way. It is at that moment that we have a "feeling" for a person, and it could probably be the moment of the so-called "love at first sight" which may not necessarily be *love* or *affection* but could go beyond that to include some inexplicable "*instinctive*" feelings or sensations in business.

Later on, the rational part of the brain, the right hemisphere, starts to make itself heard, through conditioned thoughts and contemplations related to social and cultural aspects, such as the way the person is dressed, their appearance, their race (Caucasian, African, Asian), gender and also their bank account in the worst case. At that moment our conditioned reasoning leads us to "think" about the person rather to have a "feel" for them. Listening to a voice on the radio without having an idea about the physical appearance of the speaker, is an example of how our thoughts may mislead us from reality.

It could happen that the image we have about the speaker is different when we see them on television. The person might be taller, shorter, bigger or thinner than we expected. The image of this person, whose voice we have listened to on the car radio while travelling to and from work, might shake. Thereafter, whenever we hear that voice, we will tend to associate it to an image which is different from the one we had and idealised at the beginning.

In my profession I travel a lot and interact with all kinds of people, some belonging to environments where "instinctive" love is undermined by "*calculated*" love. I find it interesting to see a couple where the woman (usually young, pretty and with a short more-or-less recognised career in show business) tells a pretending-to-be-surprised audience about her gorgeous partner (a weakthy man in his thirties or more and with a negative, rather than positive, youthful look). Can this relationship be called love? Yet, these relationships based on profits and personal benefit, have always existed. Everything is used in this earthly life to get what we desire and long for. True. But what can we expect from the feeling we call "*love*"?

Everything begins at the origin, from when we meet a person, get to know them and start to notice some aspects in them. However, some other aspects remain hidden, on purpose or because we do not dig deep enough to find out; because we do not pay attention or because we leave it to time to reveal things for us, as it should be.

Very often everything shifts to the direction of a life together in the name of love which is both *felt* and *thought*.

In other cases, you may decide to trust someone and would never doubt the truth of what they say, because everything makes us "think" that we are heading towards love. The person's gestures and glances would lead us to a path which we would later realise was not what we were looking for and would try thus to correct. In further cases, you might realise that you have not been listened to or that you have continuously been told that it was love, even if every cell in your body was screaming at you that it wasn't that because the feeling was suppressed by the mortgage contract signed at the bank, by relatives' expectations or by somebody saying "he/she is a good person."

This is the difference between feeling and thinking, and this is what it means to be aware of the consequences which might arise. I neglected this aspect for many years because I was caught up in my love of the desert and I could not understand how my "feeling" towards someone had been clouded by being conditioned and having a distorted and false perception of the person at my side.

I have crossed the harsh desert of daily life, often making thoughtful decisions, even if I felt there was something that created dissonance. It has been a great lesson from which I learned never to neglect myself and to have full confidence in the path I intend to take. It is a sentimental path which I have travelled too often with people who are attracted by the image of "*the man of the desert*", visibility and the idea of being near a person who could be interviewed or whom a documentary might be dedicated to. Those people were not attracted to me for what I am. Nowadays, I am finally and happily out of what I ironically call "*the Middle Ages*" of my sentimental life, which was the biggest misconception I have ever had. With hindsight, I can say that "I felt there was something wrong, something missing", but I was too busy with my feats, training and with rumbling, persuasive words to realise that I was condemned to fighting a lost battle and risked seeing my lifetime sacrifices, reputation and success all shatter, because I had almost blindly trusted the rationality and personality of those who I had superficially chosen to be by my side, allowing them to make me incapable of listening to my own instinct. It is incredible how the things I do and have always done in the desert are exactly the opposite, to what I did back then in the name of love.

I am grateful to that period without which, perhaps, I would not be as happy as I am today and without which, I might not have appreciated having such a wonderful family where the spirit of its members and simplicity of Love, that go beyond fame and superficiality, come first and foremost.

It was just a strenuous workout that gave rise to a great feat.

The proverb says that *"The first love can never be forgotten."* Therefore, we should never forget ourselves, being the first person to love and never to neglect. We owe ourselves respect, loving care, and lavishing attention. Besides, we have to pay attention to our body, our education and culture, and the choice of the people we meet along our journey. Some of these encounters are casual, others are desired and sought out, while others are conditioned by what we see or hear.

In any case, we should love ourselves greatly and defend this love. We should be very careful when we decide to open the doors of our heart to someone.

When we open up our heart, it is natural that we share our well-being and enthusiasm for life with the person we love and the family we start.

I used to agree with sentences like *"I love you because I need you."* Nowadays, I still stand by this, but would add the word "also" after "I love you". What I want to say is that love must not be based on a situation of need such as fear of solitude, the years that go by, and the need to settle down. We have to first fall in love, then to love each other. The months and years we live together and the children we have together, create situations of healthy "need" which become part of a solid, true love within the family.

This is why I came to the personal conclusion that the first tenth of seconds is of great importance, because it is at that moment that emotions are created before the brain starts to think.

Do you want to know what to do? I came to realise that in love we have to combine our instincts with our life experience. Trusted instinct and reason must go hand in hand, in order to avoid hurting ourselves with actions that are contrary to the so-called "*commonsense*" in our life and our journey along it. The question is: does the person we say we love have the same feelings and values as ours?. Are they really the person we think we know? Do we really know this person?

Being together, we fight to obtain something and defend it, be it an object, a dream or a thought. Being together, difficulties can be overcome with facts not only with words. Being together, we dream, laugh and even pay the bills, or else the dream will never come true. This is why I fell like saying that we are on the right way.

As far as I am concerned, I am happy and have a wonderful family that is perfectly in line with my ways of thinking and dreams.

It is very important in life to choose separate ways from those who do not have the same tendencies as us or, despite having the same tendencies, insist on "thinking" differently. I do want to point out that "way of thinking" does not mean diversities, which are fundamental for our evolution and ultimate wealth. However, dissonance is everything that drives us away from what is good for us and our own path in life.

We only have one life and we must defend it from any attempt to keep us apart from ourselves.

I reckon that life without love is like a desert without sand and is not worth running.

MY FEATS

Rules to be respected by the team during my feats:

Since it is important to gather information about a challenge, and more importantly to guarantee my psycho-physical balance which keeps me alive during these explorations, the team that waits for me at certain checkpoints, reachable by car, has to stick to very strict rules.

I have explicitly imposed extremely strict rules of conduct to be respected by all team members, including photographers, cameramen, assistants and guides. Let it be clear – and I say that again – that all the tracks I generally follow must be flawless, in a straight lines and passing through completely unexplored places where no vehicle or even camels can get to. After setting off, I may reach a track where the team would be waiting for me, let us say after 120 kilometres which naturally I will have walked single-handed. Photos and videos are taken near the checkpoint, where there is no assistance of any type, not even medical. The only exception to this can be provision of one or two bottles of drinking water. This saves me the trouble of finding well water and having to filter and disinfect it.

The rules that all members of my team have to abide by when I arrive at the checkpoint are: keeping absolutely silent, no smoking, no music, no food smells, no eating and jeep engines must be turned off. When I stop – from zero to three minutes, to pick up water, the team can quietly take pictures of me and make videos without talking to me, for as much as possible.

If it is necessary to speak, the team must talk quietly without touching me nor asking me anything and without expressing any opinion whatsoever.

There is a fundamental thing to be taken into consideration, that is, at that moment I could be running a fever of 41° and any external element that interferes with my concentration could be fatal. The team members have to whisper if they need to talk to each other.

The team must ignore any request I make because I might be delirious. The team must let me say, do things and act as I might without showing any concern about my healtheven if I stumble, fall down or faint. My levels of suffering and endurance of the heat can be misleading: five seconds after having collapsed, I could resume running as if nothing had happened. The team members must not make any decision nor take any initiative on my behalf.

The team members must not appear to be tired, unhealthy or under stress. Remember that this is an extreme adventure even for the team members! I do not have regard for anyone whilst focused on completing my mission. The team members must not take any initiatives driven by emotions. They must not search for me in case I do not arrive at the checkpoints: they could wait for me for twenty-four hours and later discover that I had skipped that point. Remember that even in the desert, I am able to run 160 kilometres per day without drinking a drop of water.

Have a nice journey

ABOUT THE AUTHOR

Max Calderan has an asset of 11 world records, and is a mental coach and sport trainer. He challenges desolate and impassable deserts reaching goals that science is still unable to explain. He has been able to achieve these outstanding results thanks to intense workouts, to spending time and energy, his spirit of sacrifice and his deep-down belief that nothing can stop our potential which has to be enhanced and used properly.

Max was born on 11th July 1967, in Italy, in the small city of Portogruaro, in the province of Venice.

He was quite a lively child and an attentive investigator. From a very young age, he started to undertake the path of young multi-talented athlete, succeeding first in climbing and extreme skiing and later reaching recognised levels of performance in more than 15 sports.

He is the national winner of the military Pentathlon. In 1988 he began his career as a teacher trainer at the same time as he became a mental trainer according to French school methods.

He dedicated himself to the study of mechanisms that regulate human body reactions to external and mental stimuli, and, in cooperation with a cutting-edge genetic laboratory in Europe, has developed a genomic test over time that makes it possible to revolutionise the concept of prevention/obtaining results today.

He is proud of having his studies published in the scientific journal "The Journal of Sports Medicine and Physical Fitness".

He has a degree in Physical Education with 110 cum laude and as a sport trainer and mental coach, he has trained hundreds of athletes since 1989 (the year he started his professional career), helping them achieve their desired goals in sport, as well as people who want to improve their physical fitness or their mind set.

He worked for nearly twenty years in managerial roles at major pharmaceutical companies. During that period he deepened his research in two areas that had always fascinated him: sleep deprivation and defence mechanisms that regulate the emotion of fear.

Max Calderan works as a professional sports consultant in the United Arab Emirates

www.maxcalderan.com
www.desertacademydubai.com

Titolo | The force within
Autore | Max Calderan

ISBN | 978-88-91149-90-9

Youcanprint Self-Publishing
Via Roma, 73 - 73039 Tricase (LE) - Italy
www.youcanprint.it
info@youcanprint.it
Facebook: facebook.com/youcanprint.it
Twitter: twitter.com/youcanprintit

Finito di stampare nel mese di Dicembre 2015
per conto di Youcanprint *Self-Publishing*

Made in the USA
Columbia, SC
27 September 2022

68054013R00078